SAS ACTIVE LIBRARY

MOUNTAIN
SKILLS

Barry Davies BEM

HarperCollins Publishers
Westerhill Rd, Bishopbriggs Glasgow G64 2QT

www.**fire**and**water**.co.uk

First published 2001

Reprint 10 9 8 7 6 5 4 3 2 1 0

© Barry Davies 2001

ISBN 0 00 710228 3

Picture credits: all images © Barry Davies, except for pp.10, 22, 27, 66, 72, 73, 74, 92, 93, 94 (top), 95, 101, 102, 109 (top), 164, 165, 177, 188, 192, 215, 237 © HarperCollins Publishers; pp. 64, 152, 160, 178, 179, 181, 182, 183, 185, 187, 198, 210 © PS5 Ltd; pp.14, 30, 82, 117, 134, 136, 139, 156, 168, 171, 197 © PhotoDisc; pp.16, 25, 32, 37, 217, © The Printer's Devil; pp. 121, 123, 127, © Edwin Moore. The publishers would also like to thank BCB International, The North Face, Vango and Petzl UK for supplying equipment images.

Material in this book first appeared in the
Collins Gem *Hillwalkers Survival Guide*

Printed in Hong Kong by Midas

Contents

Introduction

Walking in the Mountains

Planning 9
Preparation 9
Walking and Walk-leading 13
Group Leaders 14
Group Activity 15
Group members 17

Rights of Way

England and Wales 18
Scotland 20
Types of Rights of Way 21
What Your Rights Allow 22
Responsibilities for Rights of Way 22
Open Country Access Land 24
Common Land 24
Forestry Commission 25
National Parks 25
Common Problems and Obstructions 25
Conservation 43

Clothing, Boots and Walking Equipment

Overheating and Sweating 45
How the Layer System Works 45
Head, Hands and Feet 47
Boots and Footwear 48
Rucksacks 52
Keeping Clothing in Good Repair 56
Survival Clothing 58

Navigation

Ordnance Survey Maps 60
Compass 61
Orientating a Map 63
Magnetic Variation 65
Taking a Compass Bearing From the Map 67
Keeping on Course 68
Putting a Compass Bearing on the Map 68
GPS (Global Positioning System) 70

Finding Direction Without a Compass 72
Obstacles 75

Camping Out
Lodges, Mountain Huts, Barns and Bothies. . . 85
Choosing a Tent. 87
Unexpected Overnight Camp 90
Emergency Shelters 90
Sleeping Bags 95
Survival Bags and Insulation Mats 97
Cookers 98
Fire-lighting 103
Rubbish Disposal 110

Food and Water
Food 111
Water 116

Winter Mountain Walking
Fitness. 122
Precautions 122
Frozen Lakes and Rivers 123
Falling Through Ice 124
Avalanches. 126
Using an Ice Axe 128

Rock Climbing
Types of Climbing. 133
Learning to Climb 138
Climbing Fitness. 139
Equipment 140
Traditional Climbing Techniques 148
Route-finding 154
Protection 157
Knots 163
Climbing Grades 165
Descending 167

Wilderness First Aid
First Aid Kit. 171
Medical Emergencies: Evaluation 174
Medical Emergencies: Actions 176

CPR 180
Recovery Signs 183
Unconsciousness 184
The Recovery Position 185
Bleeding 186
Shock 189
Fractures 190
Burns 193
Heat Exhaustion 195
Keeping Warm 196
Hypothermia 198
Cramp 200
Blisters 201
Carbon Monoxide Poisoning 202
Drowning and Near Drowning 203
Lightning Injury 204
High Altitude Sickness 207
Forest Fires 208
Carrying an Injured Person 209
Precautions Against Things That Bite 210
Poisonous Plants 215

The Weather
Weather Problems 217
Weather Forecasts 218

Search and Rescue
Injury 222
Lost 223
Fear 223
Shelter and Survival 224
Survival Kit 225
Going for Help 227
Alone 228
Mountain Rescue Teams 230
Helicopter Mountain Rescue Operations 232
Signalling 234
When Help Arrives 238

Useful Addresses 239

DEDICATION

I dedicate this book to two old SAS friends with whom I have climbed, skied and fought side-by-side with. Their skills in the field of mountaineering were curtailed only by their untimely deaths.

Mac McAuliffe was an outstanding SAS climber and in 1969 was one of the first men to climb the formidable pillar known as the 'Old Man of Hoy'. His contribution of skills to SAS Mountaineering was unparalleled, teaching others with quiet confidence. Mac died in the early 1980s as a result of an injury he received during the Oman War.

Andy Baxter started as a novice member of Mountain Troop, but within a few years he proved himself to be an excellent climber. Having completed the Mountain Guides course in Germany, he became a member of the

Andy Baxter

second SAS team attempting to climb Mount Everest. During the ascent an avalanche swept the team down the mountainside killing one and injuring several others, among them Andy Baxter. He returned to Hereford but died of a brain tumour on the 12th August 1985.

INTRODUCTION

At some time or another most of us have relished the idea of walking through the magnificent mountainous terrain that splendours our planet. Whether to enjoy the scenery or, for the more adventurous, to challenge the towering peaks and cliffs. Whatever your reason for venturing into the mountains, you should be aware that such terrains harbour hazards and potential problems. *Mountain Skills* has been specifically designed to highlight these hazards and warn of the potential dangers. This handy-sized guide offers advice on both safe mountain walking and traditional rock climbing. While it is comprehensive it does not labour any one subject or seek to be a pure instruction book; if anything, it can be described as a logical guide, detailing how to prepare for a walk or climb and what to do should the unexpected happen.

When writing this book I drew on a wealth of experience, mainly from my 18 years with the SAS as a member of Mountain Troop. During this time I spent two years as an SAS survival instructor at the International Long Range Patrol School (ILRPS) in southern Germany. This involved teaching the basics of traditional climbing and mountain survival to jet pilots and special forces who attended the school from all over the world. Many of the courses were conducted in the Bavarian countryside, where mountain walking became part of the daily routine. On leaving the SAS I became involved with BCB International Ltd, the world's largest producer of outdoor survival products. In addition to my service with the SAS and association with BCB International

Ltd, I have also gained from personally exploring the superb landscape of America and Europe.

Mountain Skills provides up-to-date information on preparation, countryside law, climbing techniques, navigation, weather, medical emergencies and rescue. It uses a clear format to guide both walker and climber through problems that can and often do arise. No matter where you walk or climb, this book will prove an essential part of your equipment, indispensable for its knowledge and information.

Barry Davies

Walking in the Mountains

PLANNING

Any journey into the mountains, whether a several-day camping trip or just a short walk, should be planned carefully. Diligent preparation is essential to ensure that the trip is both pleasant and successful. Certain guidelines, although seeming over-fussy and restrictive, could well save a life if followed correctly. Guidelines are even more vital when a group of young or inexperienced people takes to the mountains with little or no knowledge of map-reading or survival skills. In such a case it is up to the party leader to be responsible for the implementation of and strict adherence to certain safety procedures, albeit without losing the excitement of the outing.

PREPARATION

Once the location has been decided on, as much information as possible about the area needs to be gathered. Maps, guidebooks and local people can all provide valuable facts on good, interesting routes. In particular, make sure that the location is accessible at the time you are planning to go, and that, if the land is private, you have permission from the landowner to walk across it. If you are planning a walking holiday in the mountains of a foreign country, check that the area is free of restrictions. It is best to seek permissions well in advance to avoid any disappointment. If the trip is to last more than a day, plan each day so that places of interest and targets can be reached in relative comfort.

Another aspect to consider is how you are going to get to the starting point. If using public transport, how close will you be able to get to the start of your planned walking route and is there public transport at the other  end? If you intend using private transport, remember to park carefully where you will not cause a nuisance or an obstruction (for example, avoid access routes for service vehicles), and preferably use a designated car park. Vehicles should not be taken on private roads or bridleways, or driven more than 15 m (45 ft) from a highway without the landowner's permission.

Taking into account the duration of your walk, you should consider appropriate clothing, footwear and essential equipment. If you are in a group, it is important that the group leader checks that each individual is properly prepared prior to setting off.

ESSENTIAL EQUIPMENT CHECKLIST

➤ Map and compass (see pp. 60 and 61)
➤ Boots and socks (see p. 48)
➤ Rucksack (see p. 52)
➤ Waterproof clothing (see p. 46)
➤ Spare clothing
➤ Hat and gloves
➤ First-aid kit (see p. 171)
➤ Survival kit (see p. 225)
➤ Sun barrier cream
➤ Means of starting a fire (see p. 103)
➤ Water canteens (full)
➤ Means of water purification (see p. 118)
➤ Small stove
➤ Small cooking pot
➤ Mug and plate/Mess kit
➤ Food
➤ Knife
➤ Torch and spare batteries
➤ Walking pole (depending on the terrain and the individual)
➤ extra equipment for winter walking (see p. 128)

ESSENTIAL CAMPING OUT EQUIPMENT CHECKLIST

➤ Tent (see p. 87)
➤ Sleeping bag (see p. 95)

(contd)

➤ Insulation mat
➤ Inflatable pillow
➤ Large water carrier
➤ Lantern
➤ Notebook/pencil
➤ Camera/binoculars
➤ Camp shoes
➤ Toiletries
➤ Toilet paper
➤ Insect repellent

Before setting off on your walk, check the following points:

➤ Check that you have an appropriate map as well as a compass, and that you know how to use them.

➤ Explain to the whole group where you are going and point out safety routes in the event of an emergency.

➤ Check the contents of your rucksack, placing all items such as spare clothing and sleeping bags in a waterproof plastic bag. Make sure your rucksack is comfortable.

➤ Check your clothing to ensure that you are wearing or carrying sufficient layers to cope with any weather changes. Wear purpose-made walking boots, with a decent tread and upper support. Doc Martens or trainers will land you in trouble. Your boots should be broken in and comfortable. Check you have plasters in your medical kit, just in case.

➤ It is essential that you have full waterproof clothing. If this is not worn it should be placed near the top of your rucksack.

➤ Carry enough food and water for the party, evenly distributed. Choose carbohydrate- and energy-rich food, e.g. chocolate or Kendal Mint Cake, and drinks, and don't forget your emergency rations. In wintry conditions, make sure you carry or have the means to make a hot drink.

➤ Carry a simple first-aid and survival kit.

➤ Check that no one in your group has any injuries, medical problems or allergies.

➤ Be aware when darkness falls. Wear a watch. Carry a torch (with spare batteries and bulb).

➤ The standard distress signal is six blasts on a whistle in quick succession, repeated at one-minute intervals.

➤ Make sure you know the emergency drills and signals. Don't wave at helicopters – they might think you need assistance.

WALKING AND WALK-LEADING

Whether you are alone or in a group, the walk itself should find its own pace. To hurry it too much will cause members of the party to tire and not enjoy the experience. If the route is steep or rough then a slow pace is required; if flat, the pace can be quickened, the idea being to minimise the physical effort. Walking too fast and lifting the legs over rocky or steep ground all put strain on muscles and joints, causing tiredness and aches.

The best way to walk is to find a route and rhythm where you can swing the legs forward naturally, in time with the rest of the body, including the arms, to facilitate a smooth, well-balanced action. Arms and hands should be kept free, so that in the event of a slip or fall they can be used to protect yourself against serious injury.

However, the use of one or two walking poles is increasing in popularity, especially when carrying a heavy pack, and provides additional balance and stability when descending steep slopes or crossing streams. The walker should take into account the nature of the terrain and his own ability before deciding on using poles or keeping one or both hands free.

Take extra care when climbing or descending steep slopes, and avoid scree areas. Running too fast downhill is the easiest way to cause an injury.

Group Leaders

Anyone who leads a group of people into the moutains should possess the relevant experience and skills. These skills will be a balance between time spent mountaineering and basic safety procedures learnt from study, both in theory and in practice. However, every member of the party should have some basic knowledge, especially of safety procedures and correct behaviour in potentially dangerous situations. The party leader also needs to be fit enough mentally and physically, to enable him to deal with any unforeseen problems and pass on information confidently to the other members.

Group Activity

If you are planning a long or difficult trip, filling in a route card is essential. This details the route and the proposed timing of the trip. Once filled out, the card should be left with someone who will be able to get help if you are later back than you intended. For a shorter trip or with a small party, it is not as necessary to fill out a route card, but it is still imperative to let some-one know your route and the time you hope to return. When planning a route, take the terrain into consideration and allow the time accordingly. For example, a party on fairly level ground will walk at an average 5 km/h (3 mph).

However, these who venture into the mountains will seldom find themselves walking over flat ground for any length of time. It is much more likely that they will be slogging uphill or taking it easy downhill. In 1892 a Scottish climber called W. W. Naismith advanced the following rule for working out the duration of a walk and climb:

➤ If walking normally at 3 mph (5 km/h), add 30 minutes extra for every 300 m (1,000 ft) of ascent.

Going downhill also changes the speed and duration of the walk, but in most cases the ascent and descent times will more or less balance out each other. On very steep downhill slopes add 10 minutes for every 300 m (1,000 ft) of descent, but where the ground is gently sloping deduct 10 minutes for every 300 m (1,000 ft) of descent.

The most important point to remember is that your group should walk only as fast as the slowest member. In this way you should be able to estimate the time it will take you to cover the route and therefore set a deadline for return. When considering the route, also remember to take the appropriate compass bearings and look for any escape routes or convenient shelters in the event of an emergency.

The usual position for the leader of the party to walk is in front, but this is by no means a hard and fast rule; it all depends on the type of party, the type of terrain or even the leader's own preference. Other members of the walk should be encouraged to take the lead and plan various legs in order to gain experience. What is important is that everyone keeps together and that everyone in the party knows where they are and where they are going at all times. No member of the party should ever go off on their own. During a walk, the party will need a break every now and again.

GROUP BREAKS

➤ Stop overlooking a scenic view.

➤ Check your map and compass.

➤ Keep breaks short, otherwise you will upset the natural rhythm of the walk.

➤ Only eat small amounts of food.

➤ Check every member of the party is comfortable.

➤ Warn people you intend to move off a few minutes in advance.

Group Members

From a safety point of view it is important to restrict the amount of people in any one party. The ideal number in a party is about six, and it should be no more than ten if the route is long or hard. A minimum number is three, so that if a member of the party is injured or incapacitated, one of the others can stay with him, while the remaining member can go for help. It is also important to balance the fitness, age group and experience of your party, both from a safety and an enjoyment point of view. Trying to control the walking pace where the age of participants varies greatly will cause the group to become fragmented, as the older members will be unable to keep up with the younger ones.

Rights of Way

It is important that you recognise whose land you are walking over, for example it may be private, state owned or used for military purposes. To study all the laws of America and Europe would fill several volumes and be tedious so I have consolidated those of British law to give you some idea as to what you should be looking for.

Your right of access to walk over land in Britain will depend on a number of considerations. Usually, where there is a path regularly used by walkers there is no problem, but some routes do have limited access or require special permission to use them. It is always wise to check on the legal situation first. It should also be noted that access rights differ between England/Wales and Scotland.

ENGLAND AND WALES

The most widely-known right to enjoy the countryside is that given by 'public rights of way'. All public rights of way are highways in law. Anyone may use a right of way, and may do so at any time. You should, of course, respect this freedom of use by other people, as you are entitled to expect that others will respect your own freedom of use. An up-to-date map will clearly indicate all rights of way.

AUTHOR'S NOTE

➤ At the time of writing, new laws on access to the open countryside in England and Wales are being considered. The revision is by way of a Consultation Paper which is produced by the Department of the Environment, Transport and the Regions (DETR) and distributed to all interested bodies. These bodies have been asked to contribute their ideas so that through open discussion the government can come to a balanced conclusion. Copies of the Consultation Paper can be obtained by contacting: DETR, Publications Despatch Centre, Blackhorse Road, London SE99 6TT. Tel: 020 8691-9191

➤ An equivalent process on rights of way is being undertaken by Scottish National Heritage. Recommendations will be forwarded to the new Scottish Parliament, which will consider implementing any changes. Further information can be obtained from: Scottish National Heritage, Recreation and Access Group, 2 Anderson Place, Edinburgh EH6 5NP. Tel: 0131 446-2469

➤ Powers in force at the time of writing include:The National Parks and Access to the Countryside Act 1949, The Wildlife and Countryside Act 1981, Rights of Way Act 1990, EC Council Regulation 2078/92 (the Agri-Environment Regulation)

You should not be intimidated or prevented from using a right of way. Providing you keep to the stipulated route and use a right of way properly you are exercising a right given to you by the law – not a privilege granted by the owner or occupier. It is reasonable to expect any right of way to be kept open, unobstructed and convenient to use.

It is important to realise, however, that a right of way gives only a right of passage to travel across the land. It does not entitle you to roam at will over the land, or to use the land or the path for other purposes. Remember too, that rights of way are normally just simple paths and tracks through a wood, across farmland or beside a stream. Many do not have a hard surface. They can often be muddy in winter or bordered by vegetation in summer. Sometimes a path may not be visible on the ground at all; you are still entitled to use it, but you may need a good map to be able to follow the correct line.

SCOTLAND

In Scotland the position on legal rights of way is less clear than in England and Wales. There are some similarities, however. Like England and Wales, footpaths, bridleways and highways are considered public rights of way. For these to exist in law they have to have been in uninterrupted use for more than twenty years with the owner's express permission, connect two public places and follow a defined route. However, unlike England and Wales, the authorities do not usually keep records and it is quite often difficult to establish what is a public right of way and what is not. This is slowly changing as some local authorities are attempting to draw up definitive maps. The exceptions to the above are long-distance footpaths, which are signposted along their routes and are easily recognised as common-law rights of way.

In Scotland there is a concept known as 'right to roam', a public-enhanced belief that a walker has the right to walk wherever he pleases. In reality, this has no basis in law – if you trespass and claim the 'right to roam', the courts will not recognize your claim.

TYPES OF RIGHTS OF WAY

How a right of way can be used depends on what kind of highway it is:

➤ If the highway is a **footpath** it may be used only for walking.

➤ A **bridleway** may be used for riding or leading a horse, as well as walking. Riding a bike is also permitted, but driving a horse-drawn cart is not.

➤ A **byway** is open to all traffic from walkers to vehicles.

➤ A **public path** can be either a footpath or a bridleway.

WHAT YOUR RIGHTS ALLOW

When using a right of way to travel from place to place you can, of course, stop for a while to admire the view or take a photograph. Providing that you do not cause an obstruction you may sit down by the side of the path to rest or perhaps make a sketch. You may take a dog with you on a right of way, but you must ensure that it is kept on a lead and under control.

RESPONSIBILITIES FOR RIGHTS OF WAY

The main responsibility for rights of way falls on the highway authority. If the highway authority is a county council, there will also be a district council for the area. There may also be a local community council. District and community councils have important discretionary powers, allowing them to work with the highway authority to manage, protect and maintain rights of way. For example, a district council can maintain footpaths and bridleways, can act as the agent for the county council to carry out other functions, and can initiate its own orders to create, divert or extinguish public paths. Community councils can also maintain footpaths and bridleways. They can take action against anyone who unlawfully obstructs a right of way, or they can require the highway authority to act. They can insist that a path or byway is signposted where it meets a metalled road, or carry out their own signposting and waymarking with the consent of the highway authority. Some of the most important statutory duties that a highway authority has towards rights of way include:

➤ Asserting and protecting the public's rights to use and enjoy rights of way.

➤ Maintaining the surface of most public paths.

➤ Preventing, as far as possible, the stopping-up or obstruction of any highway.

➤ Ensuring that farmers comply with the law that paths over cultivated land are properly restored after they have been disturbed (e.g. by ploughing) and thereafter remain visible on the ground, and ensuring that farmers do not allow growing crops to inconvenience the use of any right of way.

➤ Signposting footpaths, bridleways and byways where they meet a metalled road and providing additional signs and waymarks wherever they are necessary.

A highway authority's discretionary powers allow it to:

➤ Create new paths by agreement with the owner.

➤ Make orders to create, divert and extinguish public paths. Paths can be extinguished because of safety fears, new planning or because a new right of way has been established.

➤ Improve rights of way, for example by providing seats and street lighting.

➤ Provide footpath wardens.Preparing and keeping up to date a 'definitive map and statement', i.e. a formal, legal record of all rights of way.

OPEN COUNTRY ACCESS LAND

Under the Countryside Act of 1968, 'open country' is defined as land consisting wholly or predominantly of mountain, moorland, heath, down, cliff, foreshore and woodland, and land alongside canals, rivers and other stretches of water. There is usually legal public access to such areas in England, Wales and Scotland,

although certain bylaws such as the prohibition of camping and camp fires may be in force. Details of such areas may be gained from the relevant local or national park authorities.

COMMON LAND

The origins of common land date back to the feudal systems of medieval times. These areas of open land were given over to the locals, or commoners, to graze their livestock or gather wood and brush for their fires. Since the Enclosure Acts of the 18th and 19th centuries, much common land has been lost, but where it has been retained the old rights of commoners still exist. Although on most common land there now exists a public right of access by foot, bylaws do exist to control certain activities. For example, camping, firelighting and driving a vehicle are prohibited on common land. Common land in Scotland is virtually non-existent.

FORESTRY COMMISSION

As long as access does not pose any threat to its commercial interests, the Forestry Commission welcomes walkers onto its land free of charge. In some places it even provides facilities for visitors such as picnic areas and camping sites.

NATIONAL PARKS

Most National Parks permit public access on foot freely at all times. However, once again, certain laws must be followed. There are sometimes areas which the park restricts to walkers because of agricultural expediency or to protect environmentally sensitive areas of conservation. In the UK the National Trust for Scotland has far more areas of unrestricted access than its English neighbour and has chosen not to pass any bylaws on its land, preferring instead to give advice on environmentally sensitive areas.

COMMON PROBLEMS AND OBSTRUCTIONS

The responsibilities of the landowner and occupier are generally limited to respecting the public's rights of passage and to doing nothing that would inconvenience or endanger the public in any way. As most rights of way are over farmed land, provisions have been made concerning gates and stiles and to allow land to be cultivated.

Stiles and Gates

The variety of construction of stiles is part of the character of our footpaths. All stiles, gates and similar structures must be maintained in a safe condition and must not unreasonably interfere with the use of a right of way. A stile that is topped with barbed wire, or one that is dilapidated and difficult to use, and stiles or padlocked gates on a bridleway that obstruct the route for horse riders, are all unlawful and should be reported to the highway authority.

It is normally the landowner or occupier's duty to maintain gates and stiles in a safe condition. If they do this they can recover at least 25 per cent of the cost from the highway authority. If they do not, the highway authority can require the work to be done, or carry out the work itself and recover its costs. In practice, many authorities now provide free materials in the form of a stile or gate kit, which the farmer or volunteers can then install.

In repairing a stile or gate the farmer is not required to make the right of way any more convenient to use, for example by replacing a stile with kissing gates to help elderly people or by providing a dog latch to help less agile dogs. However, the highway authority or community council may be willing to arrange for such improvements to be carried out in agreement with the farmer. The highway authority's permission is normally required before a new stile or gate can be erected across a right of way. Putting a fence, including an electric fence, across a right of way without providing a satisfactory and safe means of crossing it would constitute an obstruction.

Ploughed Paths and Growing Crops

One common problem, encountered by anyone walking or riding in the countryside, is to find that the path they are following has been obliterated by ploughing or is covered by a growing crop. Important changes in the law were introduced in 1990 to help resolve these problems by making the farmer's rights and responsibilities much clearer. Highway authorities have a duty to enforce the new law and have been given strong powers do so. In addition to any prosecution they may bring, the authority can swiftly put matters right by entering onto the land and carrying out the necessary work, and then recovering its costs from the farmer.

If a footpath or bridleway runs around the edge of a field, its surface must not be ploughed or disturbed. Ploughing or disturbing the surface of a byway or public right of way is also

prohibited, regardless of whether it runs along the edge of a field or across it. If a footpath or bridleway runs across a field, and cannot conveniently be avoided, the farmer is entitled to plough or disturb it as and when it is necessary to do so to sow, cultivate or harvest a crop. He is then under a duty both to restore the surface of the path so as to make it reasonably convenient for walkers and riders to use, and to make sure that the line of the path is (and remains) apparent on the ground. Normally this must be carried out within twenty-four hours of the start of the disturbance. In the case of the first disturbance for any one crop, a longer period of fourteen days is allowed (to provide for the initial preparation of the land). Each period may be extended if agreed in advance with the highway authority.

The new law also deals with the problem of crops growing on or alongside rights of way. Crops must not be allowed to grow on, or to overhang, any footpath, bridleway or other right of way so as to inconvenience the public or prevent the line of the right of way from being apparent on the ground. 'Crops' includes cereals, rape and root crops, but does not include grass being grown for pasture, silage or haymaking.

Minimum widths are laid down for the farmer to work to, for example when restoring the surface of a footpath across a field or in keeping a right of way clear of growing crops. For rights of way across a field the minimum widths are 1 m (3 ft) for a footpath, 2 m (6 ft) for a bridleway and 3 m (9 ft) for other rights of way. At field edges, these are increased to 1.5 m (4 ft 6 in), 3 m (9 ft) and 5 m (15 ft) respectively.

You may find a right of way that is blocked (by fallen trees or rocks, barbed wire or rubbish, for example) or one that has become overgrown with vegetation. These can all be considered as obstructions and should be reported to the highway authority. The authority should clear natural obstructions as quickly as possible. It can order overhanging vegetation to be cut back, barbed wire close to a highway to be removed, and can clear anything placed or planted on the highway. If the authority has ordered an obstruction to be removed within a stated time and the obstruction is not removed within that period, the authority can remove it and recover the cost from the person concerned.

Intimidation

If anyone prevents you from using a public right of way by telling you to leave, by keeping a fierce dog close to the highway to deter you or by any other form of intimidation or harassment, you should report the matter to the highways authority. If anyone uses or threatens to use force against you, you should also report the matter to the police. You may also be entitled to prosecute privately or to apply to the magistrates to have the offender bound over to keep the peace. Committing a breach of the peace, or behaving in a way likely to provoke one, is an offence for which the penalty on conviction is imprisonment, a fine or both.

Intimidation by a Dog

It may be that you are prevented from using a right of way due to the presence of a fierce dog, either with or without its owner present. Unleashed dogs, especially those on remote farms, may well run at you and snap at your heels or lower leg. Some dogs will bite into your clothing and maintain their grip; if this is the case, try offering a padded garment to the animal (such as a jacket) to prevent being bitten. A country dog will not normally stray far from its own territory – usually the farm gate – and

you should avoid them if at all possible.

Your Dog

If you are planning to take your dog for a walk in the countryside, make sure that it does not become a menace either to other people or to those who manage the land. You can take a dog along a right of way but you must keep it under proper control at all times, just as you would in the town. You should not let it foul the right of way or farmland or any place that the public may use, and it is only common sense to watch your dog carefully on a bridleway where you may meet horses. If your dog injures a person, animal or property, you may be liable for damages.

AUTHOR'S NOTE

➤ If a dog is charging at you, try to break its momentum. This can be achieved by standing exposed next to some obstruction like a tree or the corner of a wall until the dog is a few feet away, and then at the last second moving rapidly behind the obstruction. The dog will be forced to slow in order to turn. Take advantage of this to lash out. If the owner is not present and you have no other way of defending yourself, try charging directly at the dog with your arms outstretched and screaming. Given the size of a human being in comparison to that of a dog, and the sudden unexpected nature of the attack, there is a good chance you will break the dog's spirit. A dog's confidence and security can be weakened very quickly, and while they may continue to bark, they should not come too close.

You must be especially careful in any area where there is livestock. If your dog worries them it can have serious consequences; not only are you liable to be prosecuted and fined, but you may also be ordered to pay compensation and have the dog destroyed. You should note that 'worrying livestock' means attacking or chasing any farm animal or poultry. In a field or enclosure in which there are sheep, a dog that is not a working dog can be regarded as 'worrying livestock' simply by not being on a lead or otherwise under close control. A landowner can also shoot a dog that is apparently out of control and worrying sheep, and the owner of the dog will not be compensated.

Don't allow your dog to run through arable crops or to flush out game from hedgerows or scrub. Although the damage caused may seem trivial, such actions will not be appreciated by the farmer, and can easily harm wildlife, especially nesting birds.

Bulls and Cattle

A farmer should not keep a mature bull in a field enclosure over which there is a right of way. However, there are exceptions and it is possible that you may enter a field full of cattle which contains a bull. Grazing cattle will rarely attack people who are giving them a wide berth.

However, certain young beasts may run towards you out of curiosity. Bulls have a different temperament and have in the past caused many deaths and serious injuries to mountain walkers and campers, either through carelessness or lack of respect for the bull's nature.

BULLS

➤ Wherever possible, avoid going into any enclosed space or field that contains a bull, but if you have to go in, take into account the following points:

➤ Keep to the edges and keep the bull in your sight the whole time – never turn your back on it.

➤ Before entering an animal enclosure check for sign of any bulls.

➤ If you must pass by the herd, do so at a safe distance, moving carefully and quietly.

➤ If any cattle start to approach you, shouting and waving your arms can normally chase off young heifers.

➤ Check that you have some form of escape route open to you should a bull suddenly appear.

➤ Remember to close gates behind you whenever you are walking through fields where there is livestock.

➤ Keep any dog on a lead.

Trespass

If you enter someone else's land you will be trespassing unless you have permission to be there or some form of right of way to follow, such as a right conferred by the Act of Parliament. In either case there are likely to be conditions attached to the public's use of the land, and if you contravene these you will be trespassing. Trespass is a criminal offence only in exceptional instances, so (except in one of these instances) you cannot be prosecuted simply for being in the wrong place at the wrong time. However, if you cause loss or damage you can be prosecuted (and fined) or sued (and be made to pay compensation) or both.

If you trespass persistently the landowner or occupier can seek a court injunction to keep you out. If you do find yourself trespassing and a landowner or occupier asks you to leave or to return to the footpath, you should do so. You must be allowed to do so freely. If you fail to leave, then, depending on the circum-stances, the use of reasonable force to make you leave may be justifiable.

Instances in which trespass is a criminal offence include trespass on railway and Ministry of Defence land. In addition, a law designed to deal with the problem of new-age travellers makes it an offence in certain circumstances for two or more people to take up residence on any land. In some cases, such as on some commons and local authority land, you can be prosecuted if you break the local bylaws. Remember that in Scotland, invoking the 'right to roam' is not a sufficient defence against trespassing.

If you trespass you do so at your own risk. Even so, trespassers may sue for damages for injuries sustained as a result of any deliberate attempt to injure them, or through reckless disregard for their safety. Certainly, trespassers must not be injured deliberately or threatened, and if, for example, a landowner was out shooting and continued shooting even though there was good reason to believe a trespasser might be injured, the trespasser could claim damages for any resulting injury. If the landowner threatened the trespasser with a firearm, the landowner would be committing a criminal offence.

Electric Fences

Electric fences are increasingly used to contain farm animals, especially in Europe. There are many types, including single-wire fences (often running alongside a conventional hedge or wall as a 'scare wire'), electrified nylon netting, low 'grass fences' of two parallel wires each just above the ground, and permanent electrified fences of four or five strands. They all work by sending a pulse of current along the wire every second or so. They are designed not to be dangerous but they can still be very unpleasant if you touch them. Be sure to keep your dog well away.

Use a blade of grass to check if a fence is electrified (see panel overleaf)

An electric fence alongside a public road or path should be identified with yellow warning signs at frequent intervals. Safe crossing posts should be provided on rights of way by a non-electrified gate or stile with the wires insulated, and the fence on either side also marked by warning signs. Barbed wire should never be electrified, nor should any metal that is not part of the fence itself, such as the hand rail on a bridge. If you find that any of these safety precautions are not being observed, report the matter to the highway authority or the Health and Safety Executive at once.

AUTHOR'S NOTE

➤ If you are not sure if an electric fence is active or not, it is a wise precaution to check. This is simply done by placing a small blade of grass against the fence, making sure you do not directly touch the fence with any part of your body. Hold the blade of grass in your hand and touch the tip to the fence. If you feel nothing, advance the blade of grass, bringing your hand closer to the fence. If by the time your hand is within 15 mm (0.5 in) of the fence, you still feel no tingling sensation, the fence is not live.

Crop-spraying

Spraying with pesticides and other chemicals is a widely-used method of protecting crops. They are distributed both in Americas and Europe by specially adapted aircraft and all terrain vehicles. The chemicals used to eliminate weeds, insects and fungal diseases can be dangerous to people. There are strict controls on the chemicals that are available and the way they can be used, and anyone using chemicals has a number of statutory obligations placed on them. They must ensure that the public is not endangered by posting warning signs on gates to fields that are to be sprayed. Further information should be given if there is any likelihood of the public picking fruit

from plants, bushes, etc. where the spraying has taken place.

For your own safety, do not touch or interfere with any spraying equipment (whether or not it is in use) or with chemical containers, including any that are empty. It is best to avoid walking through crops that you know or suspect have been sprayed very recently, nor should you eat, drink or smoke in the area, or pick any fruit.

If, despite these precautions, you believe that you have been contaminated, then it is usually sufficient to wash any exposed skin in plenty of clean water. Change your clothes as soon as you can and rinse them separately. If the farmer is in the area, ask for advice about the chemicals being used. Should any symptoms subsequently develop, such as trouble with your eyes, feeling sick or difficulty with breathing, seek medical advice as soon as possible. Report any problems you encounter with crop-spraying both to the highway authority and the Health and Safety Executive.

Animal Disease

You should not attempt to enter or walk across an area of land that you know to be contaminated by animal disease. You may not be putting yourself at risk, but the damage of transmitting the disease from one place to another and thus infecting clean animals is very high. The Ministry of Agriculture has the right to declare any area of land restricted if there has been an occurrence on that land of any serious communicable animal disease. In particular, foot-and-mouth disease can cause such a restriction, as happened across the UK in the late 1960s and early in 2001. In these cases even public rights of way are off limits and entering into such an area becomes a serious offence.

Game-shooting

There are areas in both America and Europe where game-shooting may take place, and where access may be restricted on certain days of the year. Mountain walkers need to be aware of these dangers which are always publicly announced far in advance, and by seeking advice from the national park authorities of the respective country. In Great Britain these are:

SHOOTING SEASONS

➤ Stags (mainly Scottish Highlands), 1 July–20 October
➤ Hinds (mainly Scottish Highlands), 21 October–15 February
➤ Grouse (moorland areas), 12 August–10 December

The Mountaineering Council of Scotland, in association with the Scottish Landowners Federation, has published a list of estates and contact telephone numbers where information about deer-stalking should be available. While no stalking is carried out on Sundays, some estates still try to restrict access then as well. Areas owned by the National Trust for Scotland are much less restrictive during the stalking season and information is more freely available. Private estates which own land where commercial hunting is carried out should also be sought out for advice on restricted areas during the shooting season. Legally recognised public rights of way are still free to be used even in an area in current use for game-stalking. However, in the interest of your own safety they are best avoided.

Military Training Areas

Almost all military training areas are clearly marked on Ordnance Survey maps as 'Danger Areas'. Most ranges, both 'live-firing' and dry combat activity, are in constant use and the walker is best avoiding them, added to which many are out of bounds during any military manoeuvres. Many access points are manned by soldiers and where they are not, standard warning notices will be displayed, with red flags being flown during the day and red lights being displayed at night. Few of these areas clash with popular walking trails, but where they do you should consult the Range Liaison Officer.

Most military training areas are well established, which means that a large amount of ordnance has been fired over the years. Some of this may have misfired and not been found or disposed of safely. Should you walk across a military training area, do not be tempted to pick up or touch any device you find lying on the ground, no matter how small. Likewise, do not throw stones at a foreign object or attempt to dig it up.

Restricted Areas

In both America and Europe there are many restricted areas which for the most part are quite small in size and situated in places that do not inconvenience the walker or climber. They are clearly marked and almost always fenced. For example, nuclear power stations (which have an armed police force for their protection) and the biological research station at Porton Down. Never try to enter a restricted area, and if you do so accidentally and are caught do exactly what the guards tells you when challenged.

Fires

Most forest and moorland fires are started by people, whether accidentally or deliberately. They cause extensive damage to vegetation, threaten wildlife and livestock, and also put human lives at risk. During dry periods extra care should be taken not to start a fire accidentally. Ensure that you do not discard any cigarette ends or matches, broken glass or bottles. Also, do not light a camp fire or camping stove unless it is safe to do so and completely under control.

Before leaving a site, check that all firebeds are cold and dowse them with water.

Remember that some rights of access such as those allowed by the National Parks may be withdrawn in certain areas when there is a very high risk of fire. Adequate warning notices will be displayed in this eventuality.

Litter

It goes without saying that responsible walkers do not leave litter behind them. It is not only unpleasant for everyone else but can also be a source of danger and contamination to wildlife.

When a trip is organised, plan for how much 'litter' you will be carrying back with you and how you will carry it back. On no account leave it behind, no matter how well hidden you think it will be.

Cairns and Stone Piles

For many years mountain walkers were encouraged to place a stone on a cairn as they passed to help build up a feature or landmark. The appearance of cairns is beginning to ruin the wilderness feeling of many routes, so don't add to them.

Trees, Plants and Wild Animals

As walkers and climbers we are merely passing through the countryside, but its wealth of wild trees and plants are the food and homes to many wild animals. Mountaineers need to be aware of the animals in their walking environment and try to keep any disturbance down to a minimum. This is particularly true of birds in the nesting season. A disturbed bird may leave the nest only to return when the chicks have died of cold or hunger, or sometimes it may never return at all. Dogs should be kept under control at all times but particularly when there are wild animals around. While you are encouraged to admire the beautiful variety of flora and fauna, it is illegal to pick or uproot any wild plants without the permission of the landowner, and some are protected by law.

Erosion

Erosion is becoming a real problem as popular footpaths feel the weight of many heavily-booted walkers, causing major problems of soil compaction and erosion. When the grass and vegetation is destroyed, the structure of the underlying soil can become unstable and will wash away in the next heavy downpour. When the path becomes so eroded, it becomes difficult to walk on and so

walkers detour off it. This then sets up the same cycle of destruction on a new piece of land until sometimes a large area can be affected. No matter how tempting it is to walk on fresh ground, stick to the footpath, and, if possible, try to tread on stones rather than soil.

Damage to Walls and Gates

 Usually, footpaths across boundaries have stiles or gates and these should be used in preference to climbing stone walls. Dry-stone walls are easily damaged, which means that livestock could escape, as well as presenting the landowner with a costly repair job. If there is no alternative to climbing a wall, ensure that any stones knocked off are replaced. Just as importantly, if you do use a gate, make sure that you close and fasten it firmly behind you.

CONSERVATION

It is vital for everyone to treat the countryside with respect and be aware that some areas are environmentally sensitive, easily disturbed or destroyed. It is up to each generation to protect what we have inherited and not to spoil our wonderful countryside for future walkers. Make yourself aware of the environment and the impact you may have upon it.

Clothing, Boots and Walking Equipment

Man is a tropical animal and needs clothes to protect himself against the British weather. The human body functions best between 96°F and 102°F; above or below this range, the person may start to decline in health. Therefore, the maintenance of body temperature and the prevention of injury are just as important to a mountain walker as the consumption of food or drinking water. Climatic temperature, wind, moisture loss, illness and shock can affect body temperature. Conduction, convection, radiation, evaporation, respiration and wind can cause heat loss or gain. This last factor is by far the worst threat in any situation, as wind chill can kill very quickly. In cold and wet conditions it can rob the body of heat, and in hot conditions it can rob the body of moisture. Most mountain walkers will tell you that getting the right mixture of clothing to suit the current climate, is a fruitless task, especially in Great Britain where the weather can be so changeable. The weather can change from hot sun to wet, biting cold rain in a matter of hours. Therefore, it is necessary to be prepared for all eventualities, so that in an emergency you will have a greater chance of survival. To guard against these factors wear protective clothing, and providing your choice of clothing is correct you should be comfortable, snug and safe.

OVERHEATING AND SWEATING

Even in cold weather it is possible to overheat, especially while wearing layered clothing. Bloodflow helps to distribute heat round the body, so be aware of any tight or restrictive clothing that may hinder this. If you're wearing more than one layer in the case of gloves and socks, make sure that the outer layer is comfortably large enough to fit over the inner. If you find yourself overheating, first of all loosen the clothing at neck, wrists and waist. If this isn't enough, start to take off your outer layers of clothing, one layer at a time. As soon as you stop exercising or working, you should put these clothes on again or you will become chilled. If the weather is wet remove one of the inner layers, always maintaining a waterproof outer layer.

HOW THE LAYER SYSTEM WORKS

The type of clothing and how you wear it will determine your body temperature. Using several thin layers will keep you far warmer than one thick layer, as they trap the warm air produced by the body. Additionally, by adding or removing a layer one is able to control the body's heat. If you are exerting yourself by walking at a swift pace, be aware that you will sweat and that the sweat will not only make your clothing wet, thereby exposing you more to the cold, but that it will also degrade the fibres of the fabric. So when doing strenuous exercise, remove some of your underlayers, replacing them once you have stopped. That way you will always have a dry layer next to your skin.

Your underclothes, that is those next to your skin, should be made of a thin, cotton material – something like a loose-fitting thermal cotton vest. This layer will absorb perspiration, thereby removing excess moisture from the skin. It is important that this layer is changed daily and washed.

The next layer should ideally be a garment that can be fastened at the neck and wrists, thereby trapping the warm air – for example, a thick woollen shirt or zip-up collar-type sweater.

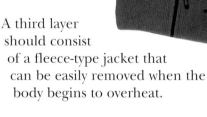

A third layer should consist of a fleece-type jacket that can be easily removed when the body begins to overheat.

Finally, choose an outer garment that is wind- and, if possible, waterproof. This could be made from tightly-woven cotton, poly-cotton, fibre-pile material or nylon. It should be

fitted with a good hood that will protect as much of
the head and face as possible. Garments made from
such materials as Gore-Tex are excellent as they allow
trapped vapour to permeate through the fabric and
reduce overheating.

HEAD, HANDS AND FEET

The head is important in both
cold and hot weather as it is
particularly vulnerable to heat
loss. An uncovered head will lose up to
a third of body heat, but this can be prevented
by wearing a head-over (a knitted woollen tube worn
around the neck) or scarf, which can be removed
from time to time in order to prevent overheating.
Although most waterproof outers have some form of
hood attached, it is still advisable to wear protective
headwear in cold conditions.

In hot weather an uncovered head can cause the body
to overheat and succumb to heatstroke, as well as
suffer from sunburn. Wearing a soft, wide-brimmed
hat will provide protection and prevent this.Feet and
hands are at the extremities of the circulation system
and so are in danger of frostbite and other unpleasant conditions caused by the cold and wet. Feet can
be looked after by ensuring your boots are watertight
before setting off. However, make sure that you do
not overdo the layers on your feet as this will hinder
circulation and make the problem worse. The same
goes for boots that are laced too tightly. To make sure
that the circulation in your feet is working properly,

keep moving and wiggle your toes every now and again. Check for any signs of numbness as this is an indicator that your foot's blood supply is being trapped. At the first opportunity change your wet socks for dry ones.

The hands need protecting from the cold and wet, and unless fully waterproof, gloves have a tendency to get very wet. In poor weather conditions cold and wet hands inhibit your ability to fend for yourself. Even small tasks such as doing up a zip become impossible. Always carry at least one pair of good loose-fitting gloves. However, unless you need to use your fingers you may prefer to use mittens.

Mittens will warm your hands far quicker than gloves owing to the amount of air circulating around your hand. If your gloves get wet a spare pair of thick socks placed over the hands will help to protect them.

BOOTS AND FOOTWEAR

The right footwear is like an old friend – it never rubs you up the wrong way and supports you when the going gets tough. A healthy pair of feet and good footwear are major requirements for those participating in any outdoor walking activity. The fact that we carry our entire body weight on two feet instead of four, like most animals, means that we place pressure on our feet. This is especially true when we are also carrying the additional weight of a heavy rucksack while walking over rough terrain. It is therefore important that you look after both your feet and your boots. Failure to do so could easily mean not completing your walk, no matter how fit the rest of your body is.

Selecting Footwear

Trail shoe

3-season boot

4-season boot

As a general rule, you should choose a pair of walking boots that combines lightness with adequate support and protection. Boots can come in a bewildering array of styles for different terrains. Good boots are often quite expensive, so most people can only afford to possess one pair. Invariably, this pair has to be able to cope with all kinds of different conditions.

Boots are made for just about every purpose. Some are better for rugged climbing, others for day walking, some are lighter and cooler for summer, others heavier and insulated for winter weather. It is up to the individual to assess their own needs and choose a boot that provides the best compromise for the type of walking they expect to do.

Socks are also important; lightweight fabric boots are designed to be worn with a single sock, while heavier boots may require two pairs of socks. In the latter case, the inner sock should be lightweight wool or silk for warmth, while the outer sock should have thickness to cushion the foot.

CHOOSING BOOTS

➤ When buying, always wear the same type of socks in which you would go walking. Make sure your toes are not touching the end of the boot. A good-fitting boot should feel comfortable, but not restrictive.

➤ Examine the boot construction and weight. (New leather boots normally need a frequent and liberal coating with wax, but they offer better support than fabric boots.)

➤ The boot backstay should protect and support the boot, as should the heel corner and toecap.

➤ The boot should be high enough to protect the ankle, with a padded scree collar and a bellows tongue to protect against water and debris.

➤ Both the insole and upper lining should be well-cushioned, giving a firm but comfortable fit to the entire foot.

➤ The boot should be waterproof.

➤ A good grip is essential, especially on wet, slippery

(contd)

rocks. Try to avoid PVC – choosing a rubber star-patterned sole will give you much better grip. The sole thickness will depend upon the sort of terrain on which you propose to walk. General hill walking does not require an extremely stiff sole, as in those used for Alpine mountaineering. Try twisting the sole to see if it is flexible. If it twists easily it will not give much support during a fall.

➤ Try to stand on an incline, or tap the heel and toe of your boot. If the toes feel trapped, try the next size up.

➤ Never purchase new footwear if you have any form of foot ailment such as ingrown toenails or corns. Wait until they have been treated.

Footwear Maintenance

It takes time to get used to a new pair of boots, so start by wearing them with the laces slightly slack and always make sure the tongue is neatly flat against the insole of your foot. Wear them around the house or go for short walks – this should iron out any hot-spots before you head off into the mountains.

Once purchased, careful maintenance will allow you to get a long life out of your boots. Clean mud from them at every opportunity then wash and polish or spray them. Any detachable insoles and wet laces should be removed and dried thoroughly using either the sun or another heat source. Beware though, of putting wet boots too close to an open fire, as leather tends to crack when it dries too fast. Instead, dry them out by stuffing them with an absorbent material,

such as paper or tissue, and leave them in a warm place. Once the boots are dry, apply several layers of a good waterproof compound, making sure that each layer is well rubbed in. Regular and careful care will prolong the active life of your boots.

Boots are expensive and a comfortable pair is hard to replace. Using gaiters that cover the entire boot will help prolong the boots' active life. This is particularly so in snowy conditions as gaiters will prevent most of the snow from going down your boots.

RUCKSACKS

Your rucksack should be large enough to contain everything you need for both planned contingencies and unplanned survival situations. This will include some form of shelter, sleeping bag, clothes, food and water. You should consider your rucksack to be your outdoor home and, like any well-kept home, everything should be serviceable, clean and in its correct place.

Rucksacks have changed in recent years, providing a level of comfort, stability and versatility to suit every kind of outdoor activity. The past decade has seen the amalgamation of technical design and modern materials such as textured nylon, two-ply polycotton and Cordura to produce an almost limitless range of high-quality rucksacks and daypacks.

Most rucksacks fall into three main categories, and within each category you will find a vast selection of makes and models to choose from. You should ask yourself what you intend to do with the pack. Once you have made this decision, you should evaluate the rucksacks available in that category.

Small Daypacks

These are designed for single-day use and are ideal if you want to carry basic day necessities such as your lunch, spare clothing, waterproofs, camera, etc. Sizes range from 18 litres to 40 litres and your own personal preference and needs should be taken into consideration. Daypacks come in different shapes and sizes, with various combinations of pockets and compartments in which to stow equipment. You would be well advised to choose a rucksack of simple construction if it is for day use only.

Specialist Packs

These are rucksacks designed for specialized use, such as climbing, mountain biking, fell-running, etc. They are for the most part soft and flexible, providing minimal resistance to body movement, although some larger packs do incorporate a very simple flexible frame which helps support the pack and its contents. Sizes for these packs are determined by the activity for which they are intended, but generally they are less than 30 litres.

Framed Packs

This is a general type of rucksack which is used by those people who intend to spend time in the outdoors, i.e. camping. Framed packs have vastly improved in recent years, with the cumbersome external frames being replaced by internal supportive structures. This makes the framed pack much more comfortable without losing its stability. Most framed packs are adjustable, allowing the wearer to tailor the pack's back-length to different clothing and walking conditions. Most people in the United Kingdom rarely stay more than two nights in a tent encampment before they encounter civilization, and this should be taken into consideration when selecting the rucksack size – 50 litres to 70 litres is appropriate for a good backpacking holiday.

Rucksacks and Weight

The spinal column supports the upper body and transfers weight downwards to the pelvis. It does this by way of a series of curves which absorb shocks and allow flexibility. The major curve is the hollow in the lower back known as the lordosis. This curve acts as a spring to take the strain, and as a result it is prone to backache. A rucksack should be designed to fit in with the body

54

shape, bear the weight it is intended to carry and remain stable. Good hip features on the rucksack, such as a wide, well-padded waist belt, help reduce the amount of strain placed on the lordosis curve. The rucksack's centre of gravity should be high on your back and most of its weight should be distributed between the shoulders and the hips. This way, your legs will help to bear the weight and your back will not get strained.

Fitting your Pack

Once you have selected your rucksack, persuade the retailer to let you fill it with some weight. This is to assess how the various adjustments found on most rucksacks react to your individual body height and build. You should also be wearing appropriate clothing. Adjust the back-length and fit any chest and waist harness, then walk around the store, checking if the pack feels right.

BUYING RUCKSACKS

➤ What will be the main use for the pack?
➤ What size do you require?
➤ Does the pack fit well? If it doesn't, don't buy it.
➤ Check out all the features, especially the load-bearing areas.
➤ Ask the retailer to put some weight in the pack and have a little walk around.
➤ Check for any pressure spots, soreness or irritation and adjust the rucksack accordingly.

Packing a Rucksack

Knowing how to pack a rucksack correctly is a skill
that should be learnt before setting out on walks. The
most important aspect is deciding what is essential
and what is nonessential. Pack a rucksack well and you
should be able to carry everything you need in
comfort. There is only one tried and tested method
which works and that is based on the principle that
you should be able to get to all your equipment with
the minimum of effort.

Items needed while you are walking, e.g. water, tea,
flasks and snacks, should be in the side pockets. If the
weather is really hot and you intend to use some form
of camel hydration system (a tube-and-water-container
contraption which allows the walker to drink without
stopping), fit it in one of the side pockets. Items of
clothing needed for foul weather should be kept
neatly folded under the rucksack top flap. Items for
use at a specific time, e.g. sleeping bag, should be in
the bottom of your rucksack, with those items that you
will use frequently closer to the top. Rain soaks
through most rucksack material and makes it heavy.
You could end up carrying an extra couple of
kilograms in a rainstorm. Waterproof your rucksack,
and seal all clothes and porous items in plastic bags.

Keeping Clothing in Good Repair

Dirty or ripped clothing does not provide good
insulation from or protection against the elements;
don't let your walking clothes fall into disrepair. The
Inuit have a very good habit of repairing clothing as
soon as it becomes damaged, thereby reducing any

further deterioration and maintaining the garment's effectiveness. It is good to adopt this bit of wisdom, especially where windproof outer garments are concerned. Never discard your clothing on a walk, no matter how warm it may feel at the beginning or how heavy and cumbersome the clothes are becoming. Never cut up your clothing for the sake of comfort. It may be hot for a few days but don't be tempted to cut the bottoms off your trousers in order to make them into shorts. The same applies to shirt sleeves. Long-term wear and tear will take its toll on any clothing, no matter how good it is. If you allow dirt to build up on your clothes, it will destroy the fibres and reduce the effectiveness of the garments. It is essential to keep your clothes clean. Washing them is the best way. If this is not practicable, a daily shaking or beating will do. Clothes worn next to the body, especially socks and underclothing, will need frequent washing and daily attention – this is essential to your health and hygiene. Many native tribes clean their clothes by simply soaking them in water and beating them against rocks. If you choose to do this, take care not to damage any buttons and zips.

When clothing gets wet, for example through perspiration or rain, its insulation properties are reduced and it will lose heat up to twenty-five times faster than dry clothing. If clothes do get wet, make every effort to dry them. This can be done by draping them over clean rocks to be warmed by the sun, or by hanging them from tree branches to dry in the wind. If possible, build a fire and dry them by that, but never leave them unattended or you might burn them. Take special care when drying leather boots or gloves by a fire. Leather, if dried too fast, has a tendency to stiffen and crack. In sub-zero temperatures, wet clothing can be hung up to freeze. The moisture turns into ice particles that can then be beaten out. This works best with tightly-woven garments.

Survival Clothing

One of the greatest dangers to mountain walkers and climbers is getting wet in a cold and windy environment, resulting in the rapid loss of body heat, leading to hypothermia, and a swift death. Survival clothing can be improvised from plastic bags, newspapers and cardboard. If you have prepared yourself properly and included in your preparations a small survival kit, you should have enclosed a large plastic bag. In an emergency, this can easily be converted into a full-length waterproof coat. Either:

➤ Cut a small slit in the bottom for your head to pass through.
➤ Cut a small aperture where your face will be if you drop the bag over your head. There is no need to cut side holes for the arms – simply keep them inside and dry.

The countryside is littered with plastic sacks and discarded supermarket bags – utilize them to protect your hands and feet. Dry cardboard or newspapers make excellent insulation to tuck around your body (always protect the chest area first), and if you need to sit on wet, cold ground use a layer of plastic or cardboard. You may end up looking like a tramp, but such improvised clothing will help keep you alive.

Navigation

Having a sure knowledge of navigation techniques will certainly help a walker to avoid ending up in a potentially dangerous situation. This section outlines how a walker can navigate by map and compass or global positioning system, as well as by more improvised (and therefore less accurate) means. There are three ways in which one can navigate: a map and compass; a global positioning system (GPS); or by using the sun, moon and stars. The correct use of a map and compass is a basic skill that every mountain walker can build upon until he is fully competent in navigational techniques. Other navigational skills, not dependent on a map and compass, can also be learnt and are extremely useful in survival situations. These basic skills will prove useful if your compass or GPS gets lost or damaged.

ORDNANCE SURVEY MAPS

A map is an essential tool to help you plan and follow a route through the countryside. Sometimes it may be difficult to see the route of a right of way on the ground, but with the aid of a good map you should be able to follow it. Although there are a number of good local walking guides, many of which contain suitable maps, Ordnance Survey (OS) maps are recommended because they show such a variety of land features as well as rights of way.

The most useful OS map to help you enjoy the countryside is a 1:25,000 scale Pathfinder map. The scale is large enough to show public rights of way in green, and other helpful information such as field boundaries. For some areas of attractive countryside, 1:25,000 scale Outdoor Leisure maps have been produced, which show additional information, such as waymarked routes, camp sites, permissive paths and some areas of open access. The 1:50,000 scale Landranger map also shows most public rights of way (in red) but does not go into as much detail as the larger-scale Pathfinder.

As well as showing those public rights of way that are on the definitive maps, OS maps show other roads, tracks and paths. Not all of these are open to the public and the map therefore states 'the representation on this map of any other road, track or path is no evidence of the existence of a right of way'. In practice, it is usually safe to assume that you can drive, walk or ride along those roads and lanes that are shown in colour on the maps, unless there are clear notices to the contrary. Some minor lanes and tracks are shown uncoloured; for this reason they are sometimes known as 'white roads'. It will usually be obvious, either from the map or on the ground, whether a particular lane or track is public or private; for example, if it leads solely to a country house or to a farm it will normally be private. Ask the local authority for advice if you are unsure.

Altitude and relief on a map are shown using a series of contour lines, which join points of equal height above sea level. Contour lines combine an accurate indication of height and a good indication of shape, and are generally shown on maps as continuous brown lines. When planning a route it is possible to follow some contour lines in order to keep a line of march at a consistent level.

COMPASS

A compass is a precision instrument used for navigation. They come in a variety of shapes and sizes, but all work on the principle of a magnetized needle which always points North. A 'Silva'-type compass is the most popular with those that challenge the great outdoors because it lends itself to the map in a variety

of ways. Most models are made of clear plastic with the compass housing containing the magnetic needle offset to the left-hand side. The base of the compass has a magnifying glass and is etched with a variety of scales. The rim of the compass housing, which can be rotated, is marked with segments showing degrees, mils, or both, while printed on the base are an arrow and orienteering lines.

Always remember that any compass works on the magnetic attraction situated close to the North Pole. Local power supplies or heavy metal objects can pull the needle from its correct course. Most compass manufacturers dampen the movement of the needle by filling the compass housing with a liquid, which sometimes produces a bubble. Providing the bubble is not large it should not affect the compass's operation.

Most compasses come with the base scale marked either in degrees or mils, or both. In a full circle there are 360° or 6400 mils. Many people in the UK, including the navy and the airforce, favour degrees, while the army prefers to work in mils. In essence it makes little difference which measurement system is used, as they both operate in exactly the same way.

However, the conversion table below should help you if you do need to swap between the two sets of measurements:

CONVERSIONS

➤   1° (degree) = 17.8 mils

➤   1′ (minute) = 0.3 mils

➤   1 mil = 3.4 minutes

ORIENTATING A MAP

When out on the mountains it is important to know where you are in relation to the surrounding landscape. This can be done by using just a map, or by using a map and compass. The procedure is known as orientating or setting the map.

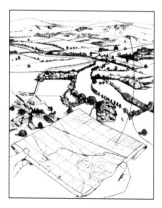

Setting a Map by Inspection

Look for an obvious and permanent landmark, for example a river, road or mountain. Find the feature on the map and then simply align the map to the landmark. The map is now set to conform to the surrounding features.

Setting the Map by Compass

Pick one of the blue or black North–South gridlines on your OS map and lay a flat edge of the compass along it. Then, holding the map and compass together, turn both until the compass needle points North. The map is now set to conform to the surrounding features.

Finding a Grid Reference

A grid reference is a six-figure number which enables a map-reader to locat an exact point on a map. When you look at a map, you will see it is covered in equally-spaced horizontal and vertical lines. These are called gridlines and on OS 1:50,000 and 1:25,000 maps they represent points which are 1 km apart. On Land-ranger maps the gridlines are light blue and on Pathfinder maps they are black. The vertical lines are called eastings: these are always given first in grid

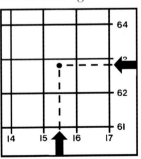

references. The horizontal lines are called northings: these are given after the eastings. Each grid square is defined by the numbers straddling the left gridline of the easting and the centre bottom of the northing.

A six-figure grid reference is worked out in the following way:

➤ Locate the point for which you would like to provide a grid reference.

➤ Mentally divide the grid square in which your chosen point is located into ten equal parts along its left-hand and bottom gridline edges. Halfway across the square would therefore be 5.

➤ Note the number of the gridline to the left of the chosen point, and then the number of the gridline below the chosen point. In the illustrated example these are 15 and 62.

➤ Working across the grid square from the left, ascertain how far across the square the chosen point is and convert its position into tenths.

➤ Repeat this procedure but this time working up the square to the chosen point from the gridline below.

➤ Placing the 'tenths' after the gridline numbers will give the easting reading followed by the northing, and therefore a six-figure grid reference for your chosen point which will be accurate to within 100 m on the ground.

➤ On the example illustrated opposite, the final grid reference is 155628.

MAGNETIC VARIATION

You should always bear in mind that when you talk about North, you could well be talking about one of three different Norths. These are:

➤ **Grid North** This is defined by the vertical gridlines shown on a map.

➤ **True North** This is the fixed location of the North Pole.

➤ **Magnetic North** This is a region in the north of Canada with a strong magnetic attraction, to which the needle on any compass will always point. However, this magnetic field is not stable and the direction of Magnetic North will vary by a small fraction from year to year, due to the movement in this magnetic field. The annual rate of change can be calculated from information which is printed in the top margin of all OS maps. You will need to know the printing date of the map and the annual rate of change of the magnetic field in order to calculate the correct current magnetic variation. Remember that the variation calculated will be that between Magnetic North and Grid North.

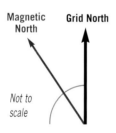

For example, if a map was printed in 1992, the angle between Grid and Magnetic North at that time 2° 30' (45 mils), and the annual rate of change is 3' (1 mil) east, the calculation would be as follows:

1992 to 1998 is six annual changes, meaning that in this case Magnetic North moved by 18' (6 mils) east towards Grid North. With an original angle of 2° 30' (45 mils), the change should be subtracted from the original difference of 2° 30' to give a magnetic variation of 2° 12' (39 mils).

To convert an original bearing, either add or subtract

the variation. The following is useful to remember:

CONVERTING BEARINGS

➤ **Mag to Grid = Get Rid** i.e. subtract the variation from your compass bearing before applying it to the map.

➤ **Grid to Mag = Add** i.e. add the variation to your map bearing before applying it to your compass.

TAKING A COMPASS BEARING FROM THE MAP

Once you have established where you are and where you wish to go, you should work out your route. Study the map and the distance. Plot the most logical route to your objective, taking into account the terrain and any obstacles. Divide up your route into legs, finishing each leg close to a prominent feature, i.e. a roadbridge, triangulation pillar or even the corner of a forest area. Take a bearing from where you are (call this point A) to the feature at the end of your first leg (call this point B). To do this, place one edge of the compass along the line adjoining A and B, making sure that the direction of travel arrow on the compass is pointing the way you want to go. Hold the compass plate firmly in position and rotate the compass dial so that the lines engraved in the dial base are parallel to the North–South gridlines on the map. Finally, read off the bearing next to the line of the direction of travel arrow on the compass housing. To walk on this bearing, simply keep the magnetic arrow pointing North over the etched arrow in the base and follow the line of the direction of travel arrow.

The bearing gives the direction to a certain point. It can be defined as the number of degrees in an angle measured clockwise from a fixed North–South gridline (an easting). The bearing for North is always zero. Compasses have scales of 360 degrees, or 6400 mils, in a full circle. Some compasses have both scales.

KEEPING ON COURSE

Three factors will determine which route you take: the weather; the time of day; and what the terrain is like between you and your final destination. In good visibility, select features which are both prominent on your map and visible to the eye. Once you have taken a bearing, choose a visible ground feature along the line of march and head towards it. This saves you constantly looking at your compass. It will also help keep you on course if the terrain pushes you off track, i.e. if you are forced to contour or avoid some obstacle. Ultimate success in reaching your final goal will depend on your route selection and not becoming a slave to your compass. Mistakes in poor visibility can be avoided if you consult the map every time you meet a prominent feature. Careful study of the map should provide you with a mental picture of the ground relief, which will in turn warn you of any obstacles, such as a river or marshland.

PUTTING A COMPASS BEARING ON THE MAP

If you become disorientated, here is a simple way to pinpoint your position. This is done by locating a couple of landmarks which can also be identified on the map. Point the compass at the first landmark and,

AUTHOR'S NOTE

➤ There is a tendency during fog or poor visibility to wander downhill when you are contouring (moving round a mountain or across a steep slope by keeping at the same height). Every 100 m (300 ft) or so, take a few steps uphill to compensate for this. Don't forget that you will move more slowly in poor visibility.

holding it steady, turn the housing until the direction of travel arrow is aligned with the magnetic needle. Now read off the bearing to the landmark. For example, say the bearing was 323° (5700 mil). Calculate the magnetic variation, say 2° 25' (40 mil), and subtract. This leaves a revised bearing of approximately 321° (5660 mil), for which the compass dial can be adjusted.

Placing the top right-hand edge of the compass against the landmark, pivot the whole compass until the direction of travel arrow in the base of the housing is running parallel to the eastings. Draw a line.

Find another landmark and repeat the whole procedure. For example, the second bearing is 37° (0650 mil), and approximately 35° (0610 mil) after adjustment for the magnetic variation. Draw another line as above. Your position is marked where the two lines cross.

Instruction in map and compass techniques is offered by a number of organizations, including local walking clubs, mountain rescue teams and specialized training centres.

GPS (GLOBAL POSITIONING SYSTEM)

This new and high-tech method of navigation is worthy of a mention, as in time it will replace the compass, although not entirely. Developed by the United States Department of Defense, the GPS (Global Positioning System) consists of twenty-four military satellites which orbit Earth, continually giving out the time and their position. Receiver units on Earth pick up this information. These units, known as GPS, have advanced at a phenomenal rate and,

although designed primarily for the military, small hand-held units no larger than a mobile phone are available to mountain walkers. The GPS unit is able to receive and assimilate information from several satellites, converting it into a recognizable position and altitude at any point on the Earth's surface. GPS units can pinpoint your position to within 15 m (45 ft) or less.

How it Works

The GPS receiver unit searches for and then locks onto any satellite signals. The more signals it receives, the greater the accuracy, but a minimum of four is sufficient. The information received is then collated into a usable form; for example, a grid reference, height above sea level, or longitude and latitude. Individual requirements for use either on land or at sea can be programmed into the unit.

By measuring your position in relation to a number of known objects, i.e. the satellites, the receiver is able to calculate your position. This is called satellite ranging. The receiver is also able to update your position, speed and track while you are on the move and can pinpoint future waypoints, thereby removing the need for finding recognisable landmarks.

AUTHOR'S NOTE

➤ The GPS requires tuition in its proper use, and is not a compass in the normal sense. In the UK I have found two models with good instructions: the Silver and the Garmin 40. The only way to learn either is to get out and practice. Despite its excellent qualities, the GPS system can be shut down at any time. In addition, the unit eats batteries, so don't forget your compass.

FINDING DIRECTION WITHOUT A COMPASS

Compasses may be the easiest and most convenient method of finding a direction, but what if you are without one? Many people wander off using just a map. This is fine until you get lost or bad weather disorientates you. Luckily there are a number of other methods for finding direction. All that is needed is a bit of intelligence.

Stick and Stone Method

➤ On a sunny day find or cut a stick about 1 m long and push it upright into some level ground (pic. 1). The stick will cast a shadow.

➤ Using a small stone, mark the end of the shadow as accurately as possible (pic. 2).

➤ After fifteen to twenty minutes the shadow will have moved. Using a second small stone, mark the tip of the new shadow (pic. 3).

➤ On the earth, draw a straight line running through both stones (pic. 4). This is your West–East line.

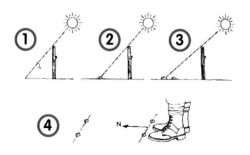

➤ Put your left foot close to the first stone, and your right foot next to the second stone.

➤ You are now facing North.

Note: The accuracy of this method depends on how level the ground is, how well the ends of the shadows are marked, and how much care is taken in placing the toes at the line. A North–South indicator can be produced if a line is drawn at right-angles to your West–East line. Any other direction can be calculated from these cardinal points.

Using a Watch

➤ For countries in the northern hemisphere, an analogue watch can be used to establish direction using the following method.

➤ Check that your watch is accurately set to local time.

➤ Point the hour hand at the sun.

➤ Using a thin twig, cast a shadow along the hour hand through the central pivot.

➤ Cut across the angle between the hour hand and the 12 o'clock position.

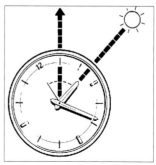

➤ This line will be pointing due South, North being furthest from the sun.

By Night

Navigation by the stars has been used for centuries, and is still employed in map-making. Learning about the stars is beneficial in itself, but this knowledge comes into its own in survival navigation. Bright stars that seem to be grouped together in a pattern are called constellations. The shapes of these constellations and their relationship to each other don't alter. Due to the Earth's rotation, the whole of the night sky appears to revolve around one central point, and using this knowledge can help you to find directions.

In the northern hemisphere, a faint star called Polaris, the Pole or the North Star marks the central point. Because of its position, it always appears to be in the same place, above the North Pole. As long as Polaris can be seen, the direction of True North can be found.

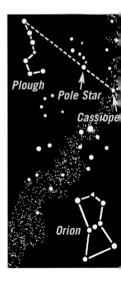

To find Polaris, first locate the constellation known as The Plough or The Big Dipper. The two stars furthest from the 'handle' always point towards Polaris. Take the distance between the two stars and then follow the line straight for about six times the distance. At this point you will see Polaris.

If you are unsure which way to look or want to

confirm that you have found Polaris, look for another constellation called Cassiopeia. The five stars that make up this constellation are patterned in the shape of a slightly squashed 'W'. It is always positioned almost opposite the Plough, and Polaris can be found midway between them. As long as the sky is clear, the Plough, Cassiopeia and Polaris remain visible in the sky all night when seen from any country north of a latitude of 40°.

OBSTACLES

Many obstacles may present themselves during your walk. Some will impede your progress, while others will influence your direction of travel. Careful route selection and good map-reading can avoid most. Study your route for large rivers, steep mountains and restricted areas. Remember, obstacles to your progress do not have to be of solid matter. Getting caught out on the mountains at night will also give cause for concern.

River-crossing

Every mountain walker will encounter a stream or small river that is easy to cross by jumping over or shallow enough to safely wade through. However, at some point you will come across a large river, or one that has flooded, which you will need to cross. Of course, it is best to avoid the situation in the first place by careful route-planning and by listening to the weather forecast. Even when confronted by the obstacle, studying your map may throw up a route to follow along the waterway on foot, without encountering too much thick vegetation, to a safe crossing place (bridge or ford). If this is the case, you should take this option.

Crossing without a rope should not normally be attempted. However, if it is certain that a crossing can be safely undertaken and if the water level is relatively low, then there are certain methods by which this may be achieved. While a group offers support and stability, there may be a situation where you must cross a river alone.

AUTHOR'S NOTE

➤ Never attempt to cross a rain-swollen river. They are deep, very fast and highly dangerous. During periods of heavy rain, the flow in rivers can fluctuate rapidly. Conversely, once the rain has stopped, the water level may drop quickly. Bearing this in mind, you should decide whether it is best to wait for the water level to drop or whether it is viable to find another place to cross safely. Crossing a stream in full spate is not a decision to be taken lightly and should only be considered as an emergency procedure, a last resort when any other decision would further compromise health or safety further.

Crossing Alone

If under normal circumstances a river crossing is deemed possible, choose the widest, slowest point, and avoid bends, as the speed of the current will increase as you wade from the inside of the bend to the outside, as will the depth of water. Wade through, rather than jumping from stone to stone. Even a simple slip can result in an immobilizing sprain or other injury – and perhaps the loss of equipment. If possible, anyone crossing should be secured to the bank by rope or safety-line. Use a solid stick as an extra point of contact and for probing the riverbed. A walking pole for extra balance is also a good idea.

If the water is slow but deep, consider swimming across. Securing your rucksack in a tightly-tied bin-liner will form an excellent flotation aid. Weak swimmers can take off their trousers, knot the wetted leg ends, grip the waistband, then swing the trousers over their head in an arc-like motion. This will trap air in the trouser legs and provide a good flotation aid.

River-crossing Techniques with a Rope

One of the most common ways to cross a river is to secure a safety-line between the two banks. This requires the rope to be taken to the opposite bank by the first person, who should also be the strongest swimmer (pic. 1). When making his way across, by either wading or swimming, he should adopt one of the methods described above. He should also be secured to the safety-line so that he can be pulled back if he gets into difficulties.

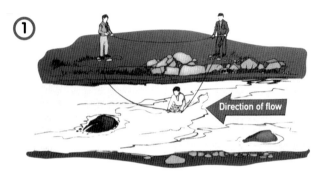

Once he is across and the line is secured, the next member (pic. 2) and each of the rest of the party should use a Karabiner (a metal hoop with screw-gate opening) to clip themselves onto the line before crossing.

The last member should unclip the safety-line and attach it to himself before crossing, in order that he may be pulled across if necessary (pic. 3). If possible, weaker swimmers should have the benefit of a second line to aid and secure them. Providing there is enough rope, a similar method can be implemented using a continuous loop.

Crossing without a Rope

To cross a river without a rope, three people should stand side by side, arms linked around each other's shoulders, with the weakest swimmer in the middle. Move across the river with the physically strongest member standing against the flow of the current. Move slowly, supporting each other in case one of the three should stumble or fall. Take care when entering and leaving the stream, especially if the banks are steep, hold onto the bank and help the weakest person out first.

If you flounder or slip in the water, it is important not to panic. If you are tied to a rope there will be someone there to pull you in. If you are using your rucksack as a buoyancy aid, hold on tight. Whatever happens, if you find yourself floating downstream, float feet first to fend off any obstacles and do not try to fight the current. Avoid any obstacles such as submerged branches, and if you feel the riverbed below you, try to stand.

Once you have crossed the river, you are likely to be cold, with your morale a little on the low side. Change immediately into spare dry clothing.

RIVER CROSSING CHECKLIST

➤ Plan your route to avoid having to cross water.

➤ Always look for a bridge or safe crossing point first.

➤ Cross only if absolutely necessary.

➤ Choose the widest and shallowest stretch.

➤ Never, unless in a life-threatening situation, attempt to cross a river in flood.

➤ If alone, use a buoyancy aid.

➤ Use a safety-line if one is available.

How to Move in the Dark

At times it may be necessary to move in the dark, especially when a member of your party has been seriously injured and requires immediate medical attention. Of course, it is better to stay put, but if moving in darkness is the only option in your situation, you need to know the safest ways of doing this.

Move only as far as you need to get out of immediate danger or to make contact, and then sit tight. To venture further when it is not necessary is to risk more injury. Although being in complete darkness can be frightening, stay calm and take stock of the situation. Check that you have no other source of lighting on you. If you are moving with other people make sure that everyone stays in touching distance with the next person. If you have a rope or lifeline, rope everyone together.

Unless a life really depends on it, do not try crossing a river in darkness – it is extremely dangerous. However, if you must, use one of the techniques described in the section on river-crossing (see p. 77). While it is a good idea to follow a stream or river on the flat, never follow water down a steep mountainside, as it will inevitably have a waterfall somewhere. Even if the waterfall is small, it will be enough to cause injuries if you fall over it in the dark.

You may find that your senses become heightened in the dark. This is good, as you can use them to your advantage. However, be aware that heightened senses mean even familiar noises may sound much louder and closer, which to some people can be unnerving – stay calm, and talk to yourself or each other if necessary.

Using the Senses

The only way to achieve 'night vision' is by waiting until the eyes have become accustomed to the darkness, and then maintaining it by shutting out any bright light source such as a torch or a car headlight. If you must look at a bright light once you have your night vision, always cover one eye to protect it.

Remember though, that low light conditions can cause the eye to be deceived, especially by distance. It is vital to use all the senses when walking at night.

MEMORY

Prior to darkness falling, you should have a good idea of the 'look' of the surrounding countryside. If your memory is good, it may aid you in finding a route out in the dark. Distance can be confusing, as you will be forced to move more slowly. Try, if possible, to locate features which can be easily identified. If you have no idea of your exact location, always move cautiously downhill as this is more likely to lead you to the safety of a road or track.

TOUCH

Touch is particularly good when it is totally dark or when you are moving over steep and rocky ground. Again, always move downhill, using your hands as if you were a climber, keeping three points in contact with the rock at all times. Use your hands and arms to make sure that the immediate space before you is clear of any obstacles and is secure to step on. If the ground is uneven or there is the possibility of a dangerous drop, crawl on your hands and knees.

SAS ACTION

➤ When I first joined the Army, I was told by one of my instructors that if I kept my mouth open during darkness it would increase my sound reception. Whether this is true or not I have always done it, and find that it does work. Likewise, during the many night operations I carried out during my SAS years, whenever danger was imminent the senses reached out into the darkness and often tingled the brain with a warning. Over the years I have learnt to accept this and become cautious when these danger signals arise.

LIGHT AND SOUND

Being caught out on a mountain during the hours of darkness does have two great advantages – those of light and sound. I know of few places in the British Isles where one can stand and not see the distant glow of a major city or the light of a small house. They may be some way off but they are still your beacon to safety. Sound can also help: metal banging on metal, the rhythmic flow of water and the noise of domestic animals all echo through the night and, if interpreted correctly, will help guide you to safety. Likewise, the sound of thunder will warn you of a coming storm, but the lightning will also illuminate the area for you, although somewhat briefly. When moving on lower ground, you will hear a river or fast-flowing stream long before you fall into it, but if you think there may be a steep drop or riverbank ahead, try throwing a stone and listen for the sound of it hitting earth or water. The sound of a search party will also carry to you, and you should always be alert to their efforts. Walking in a forest at night generally means there is little or no light. Try putting your arms out in front of you and tilting your head back to look up at the treetops. You will find there is a contrast between the dark forest and the lighter sky, a contrast that will help guide you through the forest. If you are lucky enough to come across a forest track, the same method will keep you on course. As there are no trees on the track, there will be a clean edge to the treetop silhouette.

When walking over snow-covered ground on a clear night, the starlight and moonlight will reflect off the white surface. However, should it start snowing hard or if the wind is blowing a gale, you should reconsider your night movement, as progress in a blizzard is life-threatening: moving in a blizzard has a disorienting effect and pitfalls below the surface are obscured. However, on a clear moonlit night it is possible to see for up to 100 m and you should be able to look up and identify the various star constellations. The Pole Star will give you an approximate northerly direction and thus all other points of the compass can be worked out (see p. 74).

Camping Out

If you intend to camp out during your walks, you will need to consider where you are going to sleep and, more importantly, how you are going to protect yourself against the elements. In the more popular walking areas in the UK such as the Lake District, Peak District or Brecon Beacons you can always find a wide variety of homes and farms offering bed and breakfast. However, if you prefer the isolation of the mountains or the tranquillity of the valleys, you may prefer to camp out or use a bothy.

LODGES, MOUNTAIN HUTS, BARNS AND BOTHIES

Many of the mountain ranges offer respite in the form of lodges and mountain huts, some of which are permanently occupied on a commercial basis. This is particularly true in Europe where the mountainous regions have large centres of population in the nearby valleys. For example, you can climb a horrific ice wall in Chamonix, France only to emerge at the top to find a packed restaurant. Many of these lodges offer overnight staging posts prior to completing the early morning walk to the summit, as at Mont Blanc.

Bothies, mountain huts, barns and derelicts are a

totally different thing. Most are little more than old abandoned country dwellings which provide a ready-made shelter for the mountain walker in remote areas. In many areas they have been renovated to the point where they will keep the wind and rain out, and a few are provided with fuel and a fireplace. To the weary walker they provide simple accommodation (in most cases free) but you are expected to provide your own sleeping equipment and cook your own food. If you do use such a building, remember those that come after you, and leave the place as tidy as you found it. Do not be tempted (unless it is an emergency) to use buildings intended for animal use, as they will contain droppings and will be crawling with lice and ticks. Contact the Mountain Bothies Association for details of bothies in the UK.

Camp Sites

The more traditional way of camping out is to use a tent, either pitched in a recognized camp site or in a permitted area. If you are not sure where to camp, it is always best to ask the local landowner for permission. Most appreciate the gesture and will

indicate a good spot. Pitch your tent carefully, with the tail/back end facing into the wind. Select your site carefully – for example, away from damp ground or too close to a river. Mist will collect over the water during the early morning and your tent will get very damp if you are too close. If you find yourself on wet ground or think that it will rain in the night, pitch your tent on a small mound where the ground will carry excess water away. Don't be tempted to dig drainage ditches around your tent. The site owner or farmer will not appreciate it, and in most cases a ditch will merely hold the water around your tent.

After a while, camping in the same spot can have an impact on the ground. Moving your tent every two to three days will avoid damage to the underlying vegetation. Be sure to clear the camp site of litter.

CHOOSING A TENT

Even if you have not planned on camping out, there are other reasons for carrying a small tent. The weather may suddenly turn nasty, forcing you to seek shelter, or a member of your party may be taken ill and require the protection of a tent. Tents keep out the wind and rain, while keeping the warmth in. In an emergency most modern tents can be erected in a matter of minutes.

You will find a wide variety of tents available, ranging from a few pounds to several hundred, the price reflecting the quality and style of tent and its intended usage. There are tunnel tents, hooped tents, dome tents, ridge tents, and so on; as a mountain walker you should choose a tent to suit your needs. Consider what sort of weather you are likely to be camping out in. For British conditions you will

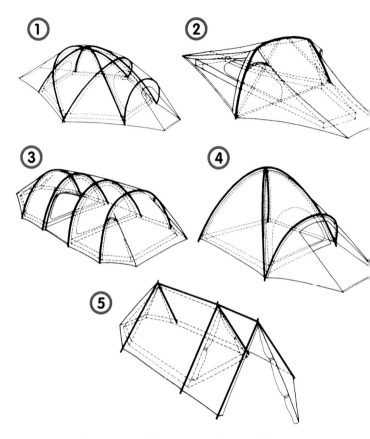

Tent styles: (1) geodesic (2) hoop (3) tunnel (4) dome (5) A-frame.

require a fully weatherproof tent with some form of porch in which you can cook and store your rucksack. When choosing a tent you should ask yourself certain questions and always buy the best quality tent within your budget. Most tents are supplied with a stuff sack, which will house the lightweight flexible poles, tent and flysheet if separate.

Cotton tents do not suffer from condensation problems but are prone to getting wet, which makes them hard to dry and heavier to carry. All nylon tents are lighter and fully waterproof but suffer badly with condensation. A good compromise is to choose a cotton tent with a waterproof groundsheet and a nylon waterproof outer. Gore-Tex tents are another option, as they are light and breathable, but very expensive. Tents can be costly so always make sure that when you return home your tent is put out to dry to prevent it becoming mildewed and rotten.

CHOOSING TENTS

➤ How large should it be, and will you be sharing it with someone else on a permanent basis? Sharing cuts down weight, especially if the tent comes in separate parts.

➤ Weight. Ideally your tent, complete with outer flysheet, should not exceed 4 kg (9 lb) for two people, and half that if you camp alone.

➤ Insects can be a real problem, so make sure the tent entrance has a well-fitted insect screen.

➤ Consider where you will be camping. Dome tents with a large inner volume may not be very stable when positioned on a high windy plateau.

➤ Tents can be very bland in colour. Don't forget that your tent may have to be used in an emergency, so despite what the conservationists say, choose a bright colour.

➤ If you want serious lightweight camping you might try a bivvy bag.

UNEXPECTED OVERNIGHT CAMP

An unexpected incident can occur at any time and may well make it necessary for you to spend a night outdoors. Providing no one is injured, and there is no real emergency, such a situation will test all your skills of improvisation and add to your mountain walking experience. In reality you should have about your person some form of minimal survival kit (see p.000). However, you may have only what you stand up in. If you are alone you must formulate your own actions, but if you are in a group you must rely on the judgment of the party leader or senior.

EMERGENCY SHELTERS

If you find yourself in a survival situation – a situation in which something unexpected has happened or your safety is put in jeopardy – you should decide on the order of priorities, and where the need for shelter lies within that order. For both mountain walkers and climbers, the need for shelter will come from an injury or the need for protection against the weather. The most dangerous conditions include cold, wind, rain and snow, as each of them is a factor which hastens hypothermia. Exposure to any combination of these can produce fatal results long before any shortage of food or water will take effect. Even in summery conditions or hot climates, shelter from the sun is needed so as to avoid overheating of the body. It may not affect the survivor as rapidly as loss of body heat, but it can still be deadly, as it will very quickly lead to a loss of body fluids.

Choosing a Site

Using a survival sheet as a makeshift shelter

Caught without a tent or emergency survival bag, temporary shelter is quickest found among the natural features surrounding you. Seek it in or around trees, thick bushes or natural hollows. If they are safe, make use of caves, rock overhangs or any available natural shelter. Never waste time and energy constructing a temporary shelter or windbreak if nature or circumstance already provide it. Choose the best site that gives natural cover from the wind. If no such cover is available, consider making a windbreak. If you are likely to be in the position for some time, construct a shelter as near as possible to sources of building materials and, very importantly, firewood. Any spot in a forest and near a fast-flowing stream can be the site for a good temporary camp.

WARNING

➤ If you are forced to camp in lowlands during heavy rain, beware of possiblefloods. On the coast also keep the tides in mind. In mountainous areas make sure that the chosen site is not in the path of possible avalanches or rockfalls. If you are in the forest, look around for fallen trees which may indicate that it is an area of shallow soil. If high winds can blow one tree over, it could do the same to others nearby.

EMERGENCY BUILDING
MATERIALS

➤ **Sheeting** Any type of sheeting can be utilised for shelter; groundsheets, plastic sheeting, sacks, canvas or blankets.

➤ **Turf** Turf can be used for construction on very flat open areas where trees and shrubs are scarce. In many countries it is used as a roofing material. If you don't have a knife for cutting turf, a flat, sharp-edged stone may well suffice.

➤ **Foliage** With foliage it is possible to construct an excellent long-lasting waterproof shelter. Where available, use large-leafed foliage.

➤ **Rocks and Stones** Where the ground is hard or foliage is in very short supply it will be possible to make a good shelter out of rocks and stones.

➤ **Snow** If you are caught out in wintry conditions, and the depth allows it, snow can be a good source of building material.

Forms of Quick Shelter

Lean-to Frame

The lean-to frame is the standard shelter pattern, probably because it is one of the simplest. When setting up the frame, make sure that the roof slopes down into the prevailing wind. The covering can be almost anything, from foliage to plastic sacks or a groundsheet – even turf

blocks can be used. A firm mud or turf layer on top
of foliage will harden, preventing the shelter cover
from being blown away and making it more wind- and
waterproof. The sides of the shelter can be filled in
using a similar foliage-and-mud method or could be
walled with turf blocks.

Tree Bivouac

A small shelter can be made quite quickly using any
small tree. Cut part way through the trunk at a point
about shoulder-height until you are able to push the
upper portion over so that its top rests on the ground.
The stem should be left attached to the butt. Cut away
the branches on the underside and break the
upstanding
branches on the
outside so that
they hang down.
Thatch the shelter
using the foliage
cut from below.

The Snow Trench

A hole in the snow provides temporary shelter as an
emergency measure, and it can be improved to make
a simple shelter for one man. If the snow is soft,
branches or sheeting of some kind will be needed for
the roof.

The Fir Tree Snow Shelter

If you are in a wooded area, by far the simplest shelter

can be found under a large fir tree. There will often be a natural hollow in the snow around the base of the tree trunk to give you a good start. Dig away the snow from the base, using it to build up and improve the protection on either side of the shelter area. Cut away the low branches on the side to use either as bedding or to interweave with the branches on your side to improve the overhead cover. You can build a fire under the tree, but make

sure it is at least part of the way around the trunk from your shelter. This is because the heat will melt the snow in the branches above the fire. This type of shelter can be readily made in forests during summer (even when there is no snow) and winter. The foundation provided by nature needs only slight improvement to make it warm and comfortable.

The Snow Cave

This type of shelter requires a depth of snow of 2 m (6 ft) or more. The simplest approach would be to build into a snow drift or cornice. To improve the snow cave, aim for as many of the features shown in the cross-section as you can. Sometimes this type of shelter is more difficult to make than it

appears, because of the hardness of the packed snow. Without some tools it may be impossible. Make sure that the inside roof is always dome shaped, or you will wake up in the morning with it on your head.

SLEEPING BAGS

We spend a third of our day sleeping, and even more when camping out, as we go to bed earlier and normally want to remain in our cosy bag just a little bit longer. For this reason it is worthwhile choosing a good-quality sleeping bag. There are many different types on the market and there are only two real elements to look for: warmth and construction. Weight is also important, but for the average person many of the sleeping bags you look at will be of very similar weights.

Warmth is the most important factor and the argument over which is the best filling, duck down or synthetic, still goes on. The answer is neither, as it is the air trapped inside the insulation and not the material that keeps you warm. In very general terms, the more loft (thickness) a sleeping bag has the warmer it will be. Synthetic is cheaper and has the advantage of not losing its insulation properties when wet. Down, on the other hand, is lighter and can be compressed into a much smaller space, but collapses when wet.

The construction of the sleeping bag is also important. Cheap oblong bags with a wraparound zip are little more than a folded blanket. A mummy-shaped bag is warmer simply because there is less space for your body to heat. You should also choose a sleeping bag that has a hood, as 80 per cent of your body heat escapes from your head.

Likewise, a sleeping bag with a boxed foot section will help you feel comfortable and unrestricted.

AUTHOR'S NOTE

➤ If your build is short and you find that your sleeping bag is too large, try shortening the bag by sealing off the bottom with a waist belt or tying a piece of cord around it. This helps cut down the amount of wasted space around your feet, thus increasing the temperature and heat retention inside the sleeping bag.

CHOOSING A SLEEPING BAG

➤ The sleeping bag should not be too large.

➤ It should have a draught strip behind the zip to protect against warm air leakage.

➤ It should have a hood and a foot box.

➤ The zip should be operable from both inside and out.

➤ The filling should be appropriate to your needs.

➤ The stitching should be of a high quality.

SURVIVAL BAGS AND INSULATION MATS

Every person who ventures into mountainous terrain is advised to carry at least one survival bag as part of a survival kit, or in the flap of a rucksack. Survival bags are invaluable as they can provide shelter from both wind and rain. They come in a variety of sizes, colours and thicknesses, but all serve the same basic purpose.

A Camo-Glo is two large, strong polythene bags, one of which is placed inside the other and the cavity filled with dry straw, leaves or grass, to form an insulated emergency bag. A good survival bag will act as a sleeping bag or can be converted into a simple tent.

Some survival bags even have emergency instructions printed on the front.

Insulation mats have been around for many years and they provide much-needed protection from ground that's cold and damp. Most modern sleeping mats are made from specially-laminated EVA closed-cell foam. They vary little in size, normally being some 20 cm (8 in) wide and 60 cm (2 ft) long, and come either rolled or folded. Insulation mats are extremely light-weight, cost very little money and are excellent value.

COOKERS

There was a time when all the camper needed was a small camp fire. This would provide heat for cooking, light and a modicum of comfort. However, in addition to leaving a permanent scar on the earth, open fires, especially in summer, pose a huge risk to forests and dry grassland. Moreover, modern camping cookers are convenient, as they do not need a continuous supply of dead wood, are simple to light and control, and, although it is not recommended, they can be used indoors.

There are two types of cooker, solid fuel and liquid fuel, the main difference being regulation and control of the heat source. Solid-fuel cookers have been around for over two thousand years in one form or another and they are simply a brick-type block of fuel that burns in a container and acts as a cooker. Modern-day variations use a small tablet, usually constructed of Hexamine, placed on a small folding metal cooker on top of which a pot is balanced. With a little practice, solid-fuel blocks are simple to light. However, they do need protection against the wind. The solid-fuel cooker has the drawback of allowing the flame to penetrate through to the ground, so consideration should be given to the placing of your cooker in order to prevent forest fires.

Liquid-fuel cookers fall into two main categories, gas- and petroleum-based mixtures, the difference being the burning time and pressurization. Petrol- and kerosene-type cookers normally require pressurization and they have a much shorter burning duration when compared to the weight of gas cooker fuel. Gas cookers such as propane and butane do not require pressurization, are lighter and have a longer burning time. They also have fewer moving parts which makes maintenance much easier. Both types are produced in a range of sizes, and are convenient to light and use. Fuel for petroleum-based mixtures is readily available worldwide, whereas the small individual gas containers and solid-fuel cookers are generally restricted to camping outlets.

Cooker Safety

If used carefully and the manufacturer's recommendations are adhered too, all forms of camping cooker are relatively safe. Fuel spillage, over-pressurization and fuel canisters not fitted properly are the main causes of flare-ups and dangerous mishaps. Badly placed cookers and unbalanced cooking pots also present problems resulting in scalding and burns. It is for this reason that camping cookers should not be used in a tent or confined spaces. Many people construct a reflective shield in windy conditions. Providing this is done properly there is no problem. However, using a shield constructed of flammable material, or placing the shield too close to the cooker, can cause overheating. If you are using a shield and your cooker is fitted with a pressure release valve, make sure it is pointing away from those doing the cooking.

Gas cookers require the removal and replacement of gas-filled cartridges. In the main this is extremely safe but you should do it in the open and away from any naked flame. New cartridges should not be exposed to heat or left in direct sunlight, and old cartridges should be disposed of in a responsible manner.

Carbon Monoxide Poisoning

Carbon monoxide poisoning can easily occur if you burn a fire or a stove in an unventilated place, such as a tent. The gas is colourless and odourless – once you realise that you are being poisoned, you may lack the energy to escape. It is best to be aware of the dangers and make sure that you have adequate ventilation, and that the flame on your stove burns blue instead of yellow. The symptoms are headache, lethargy, confusion, nausea and vomiting, followed by distressed breathing and loss of consciousness. Get the casualty into the fresh air as quickly as possible. Put out the offending stove or fire and ventilate the tent (see also p. 202).

Improvised Cookers

If you find yourself without a cooker or you are in a survival situation, it is not too difficult to improvise one. For a heat-source required for a short period of time you are best building a small fire surrounded by a ring of stones to prevent it spreading. Cooking on an open fire is not easy, as the food has a tendency to burn on the outside and be uncooked on the inside. A simple improvement is to construct a basic stove.

Billycan Cooker

This improvised cooker is constructed from a large metal can. The size of the can is fairly immaterial but a large catering-sized bean can is about right. Using any available metal can or box, it is a simple matter of punching a few holes in the base and around the bottom of the tin. This will provide the air required to make the fire burn. Other small improvements can be made by cutting down the lip a few inches and bending the metal inwards to form a stand on which you can rest your cooking pot. This type of cooker is economical as far as fuel is concerned (anything  non-toxic that will burn can be used), and is well-suited to colder conditions, since, with care, it could be used inside a shelter (but not a tent). Additionally, the billycan cooker may be carried once it has cooled down.

Yukon Stove

The Yukon stove is a simple and safe way of building a fire and utilizing its heat. If you are in one location for more than twenty-four hours, and the ground and regulations allow it, you should certainly seriously consider building this type of stove.

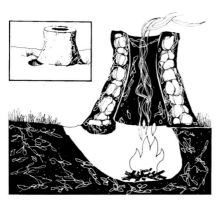

The Yukon stove normally takes about two hours for one person to construct, providing most of the materials are to hand. It requires only rocks, stones and mud for its construction, fashioning a hollow tortoiseshell hump as the basic design. At one side you must leave a hole for the intake of fuel and air, with another at the top to act as a chimney. Two further refinements are very desirable. The first is the building in of a metal box or large can into the back wall. This will provide an excellent oven. You must remember, however, that food placed in the oven will be burned unless it is separated from the metal by small sticks or stones. If twigs are used they will turn into charcoal after a day or two. You should keep this for use in deodorizing boiled water if necessary, and for other medicinal purposes. The second improvement is to use a large flat rock as part of the top of the stove, which can be used as a griddle.

One of the Yukon's major advantages is that it can be left unattended while you are working at other activities. Wet clothing can be laid over the outside of the stove and will dry without burning. You can also warm yourself without risk of being burnt.

FIRE-LIGHTING

Fire is one of the essential aids to survival, and the ability to light a fire in difficult circumstances is a survival technique of inestimable value. Fire will provide heat and light, together with the ability to cook food, purify water and sterilize medical equipment. Clothing can be dried, and signals can be generated, thus seeking help. Fire is a powerful tool.

CARE WITH FIRES

➤ Only light a fire where necessary, for, although a camp fire can be enjoyable, out of control it can also cause great damage to the local environment.

➤ Make sure that you locate such a fire in a position where it cannot do much damage, and be careful about using certain rocks, such as limestone, as when heated these have a tendency to explode.

➤ Collect only dead wood for fuel. Never cut live wood, but bear in mind that even dead wood has an important role in the natural cycle of regeneration so only take as much as you need for a small fire.

➤ When leaving the site, ensure that the fire is completely out, the ashes cold, replace any rocks used and try to eradicate as many traces of the fire as possible.

The Basic Elements

Any fire requires three elements: heat, fuel and oxygen. If any one is missing, a fire will not burn.

Fuel

When considering the supply of fuel, it is helpful to recall that fire is a form of chain reaction. Part of the heat generated by the combustion of any fuel is required to ignite the succeeding supply. The initial supply of heat available to start the fire is usually small – a match flame or spark which lasts only a few seconds. It follows that the starting fuel, which must be set alight by such a brief flame, must be a material that ignites very easily. This form of fuel is referred to as tinder. Tinder must be dry, so that it will ignite readily. It is therefore essential that, before attempting to set light to the tinder, you make certain that there is a supply of kindling ready to hand. Kindling will consist of small dry twigs, followed by dry sticks, which will enable a small, hot fire to be built. You may then gradually add larger sticks until you have a fire which will burn long enough to ignite small logs. When such a fire has been established, even green logs can be added, since the heat available will boil out the sap long before the logs burn. At first, however, the wood you gather should be dead, and as dry as possible.

Before you attempt to light your fire, it is essential to collect, grade and stack the fuel into tinder, kindling and heavy fuel. Be sure to gather sufficient quantities to build and establish your fire. It is also very

important not to fall into the common error of piling
kindling and other wood onto the fire too soon.

Doing so will probably limit the supply of oxygen and
the fire will die. If you ensure that the fire is well
ventilated, it will burn efficiently, and the smaller
wood will produce less smoke.

Heat

The heat required to start a fire can be generated in a
number of ways. The easiest to use is an open flame,
from a match or lighter. Sparks from flint and steel,
or from an electrical source, can be used to ignite
tinder. A magnifying glass or parabolic reflector, in
sunny conditions, can do the same. Friction is a good
source of heat, but it is the least preferable of these
methods owing to the amount of effort and time
involved. Details of the various heat-sources are given
later in the section (see p. 107).

Lighting a Fire

It is well worthwhile taking some care when choosing
a site for your fire. If you have, or are going to build,
a shelter, you will not want it to be filled with smoke.
On the other hand, heat from the fire should be
available within the cover.

Once the fire is established, it is often useful to
enclose it in a circle of stones, if they are readily
available. This will define the size of the fire and
lessen the danger of it spreading. If larger stones are
used on the windward side, the fire will be able to

burn more steadily than if it were entirely open to the wind. This is important, because a continually fanned fire consumes much more fuel than one that is sheltered. Gathering wood for a roaring fire can use up a great deal of time and energy.

FIRE POINTERS

➤ Choose and prepare the site for your fire.
➤ Check the wind direction, and the dryness of the location.
➤ Look at the availability of fuel in the area.
➤ Gather your fuel supply and sort it into categories.
➤ Prepare the tinder.
➤ Light and build the fire – slowly. Do not smother it.
➤ Provide the fire with good ventilation once it is started.
➤ If conditions are windy, some form of shield must be erected or provided before attempting to light your fire.

A fire may appear to have burned out overnight. If so, check the ashes and embers, as they will often retain enough heat for you to be able to relight your fire from them. If the ashbed feels warm, gently push some tinder down into the ashes. Use a twig to do this or a burned finger could be the result! Once the tinder starts smoking, gently blow or fan into flames, and add tinder required to relight the fire. Always keep a good supply of fuel to hand, and perhaps an adequate amount of earth, sand or water to control the flames if necessary.

> **TINDER SOURCES**

➤ Decayed or powdered dry wood
➤ Pulverized outer bark (cypress, cedar, birch)
➤ Crushed cones from evergreen trees
➤ Any old nest material (rat's, bird's, etc.)
➤ Scorched or charred cloth, especially linen
➤ Cotton wool (best covered in charcoal)
➤ Some photographic film
➤ Charred rope, lint from twine, canvas, bandages, etc.
➤ Petrol or cooker fuel
➤ Insect repellent
➤ Oil

The last three in the above list should be used in conjunction with some solid form of tinder, or poured over sand or absorbent material. All tinder obtained from solids is most effective if it is reduced to shreds, threads or fibres and loosely piled to ensure good ventilation with enhanced combustibility.

Heat-sources

Heat can be obtained from many sources, and in cold climates the ability to produce a flame is absolutely essential for survival.

Matches

Always carry a supply of matches as a matter of

 course on all outdoor trips, for they are the easiest and most obvious means of generating flame. They are, however, vulnerable to the effects of damp. Matches can be protected from water by dipping each separate match into molten wax, covering the head and half the stick. Spraying it with hair lacquer can protect the outside of the box.

Special wind- and waterproof matches can be purchased from most camping outlets. These are not expensive and will provide a constant flame for about six seconds in the worst weather. Always aim for One Match, One Fire.

Lighters

A lighter can be a lifesaver. It does not suffer the effects of damp and will generally light over two hundred fires. Even when the lighter fuel is eventually exhausted, don't forget that sparks from the flint can be used, with tinder, to light a fire.

Candles

A candle, however small, will prolong the active life of your matches or lighter, besides helping you light the fire. This is because most people can light a candle with one match or first time with a lighter. You then have a constant naked flame to ignite the tinder, even if it is slightly damp.

To put this technique to use, cut a small hole in the ground or build a small shield of stones around the candle. Pile the tinder over the hole or shield, and slide the lighted candle underneath. As soon as the tinder starts burning,  remove the candle. This is a particularly good method of lighting a fire if it is raining or the fuel is wet.

Flint and Steel

This is one of the cheapest and better items on the market. Developed for the military, it consists of a 5 cm (2 in) flint which is stroked by a serrated hacksaw blade, producing a large amount of sparks. Properly used, a flint and steel will light up to two thousand fires, irrespective of being wet or dry.

 A similar product is an aluminium block impregnated with magnesium housing the flint along one of its edges. The sharp edge of the hacksaw blade will first produce shavings from the block. These can then be ignited with sparks struck from the flint. The heat produced is brief but the heat output of burning magnesium is in excess of 2700°C (5000°F). This item

of firelighting equipment is highly recommended for inclusion in any survival kit.

RUBBISH DISPOSAL

Most people understand the value of the countryside and never drop litter. However, one does not have far to walk into the mountains before some form of can or wrapper can be found. Some rubbish can be burned in your camp site, while nontoxic liquid may be disposed of in an open pit well away from any water supply. Be very careful how you dispose of plastic bags and polythene as they are particularly lethal to animals. The best advice is to take your rubbish home and dispose of it in a proper refuse bin.

Food and Water

Eating in the outdoors is a pleasure akin to the mountain walking itself. There are few things better than stopping for a cup of tea and a sandwich at lunchtime while overlooking some magnificent scenery.

FOOD

However, it is not just a matter of eating – it's also a matter of what we eat. Mountain walking and traditional rock climbing require a lot of physical effort with an average usage of around 3,500–4,500 calories per six-hour walking day. The body derives its energy from what is eaten, and stores energy in the form of fat and carbohydrates. Fats release their energy slowly and only when the carbohydrates have remained low for a period of time, i.e. when an activity is burning more calories than the body is consuming. The carbohydrates, which are stored as glycogen in the muscle, provide the energy to meet the immediate demands placed on the body through vigorous exercise. As the glycogen is depleted the body becomes exhausted and the need arises to rest and replenish our energy by eating food.

The best advise is to eat a normal diet but make sure

it is rich in carbohydrates, with average protein levels and low fat. This can be achieved by purchasing fresh food and making your own menus, or buying ready-made camping meals. There are many points for and against: tinned food is heavy; fresh food is healthy but has a fixed shelf-life; freeze-dried food is light but needs reconstituting. How you eat and what food you eat will depend on whether you intend to camp out or return to your accommodation each night. In accommodation where breakfast and an evening meal are provided, a simple bag of sandwiches and fruit, together with a flask of hot drink, is sufficient. However, you should not forget to pack at least one extra day's food to carry you through any survival situation. This should not be pilfered to supplement your day's food.

The range of outdoor camping food is vast and comes in a variety of forms. Your choice should be made taking into account the length of stay outdoors and the difficulty of the walk, with the main emphasis being placed on weight. It is a good idea to balance out any tinned or packet food with a supplement of items such as bread, and fresh vegetables such as onions, tomatoes, etc. (only take fresh food that can be eaten raw or after a small amount of cooking). Fresh eggs can be carried for breakfast. Break them into a large-necked polythene bottle with a good screw top. This way you can pour one or two eggs into a pan for cooking. They will last up to three days.

Wet Packs

These contain normal cooked food as one would find

in a tin, but packed in a foil pouch or tray. Their only advantage over cans is the packaging. You will still be required to carry the water weight held within the food, as the difference in

weight between a can and the foil pack is minimal. Some wet-pack foods can be cooked in their transit containers. However, it is best to put the contents into a proper cooking pot to avoid burning the bottom.

Freeze-dried Food

This type of food has improved dramatically over the past few years and is ideal for camping due to its light weight. The packs contain 96 per cent real food, as opposed to 80 per cent water in wet foods. They are normally packed in a foil pouch which enables boiling water to be added, thus reconstituting the contents hot in the bag. The food can also be cooked normally on a heat-source and by adding water. Menus include breakfasts, main meals and desserts, and an excellent vegetarian choice is available. Meals take about five minutes when cooked in the pack and about seven minutes when cooked conventionally. Freeze-dried food has a shelf-life of up to three years.

Heater Meals

These are pre-cooked food that is packed in a plastic tray and foil-sealed. The meal comes with a water-

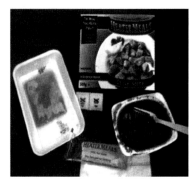

activated heater unit complete with a small sachet of water, fork, napkin and salt and pepper. The meal takes about fourteen minutes for it to become hot. Heater meals have a shelf-life of one and a half to two years.

Hot Cans

These are cans of food which can be cooked without the need for fuel. This is done by puncturing a water-activated membrane surrounding the inner can in a similar way to the heater meals. They are, however, very heavy, with a food weight of 425 g (15 oz), and an overall weight of 870 g (30 oz). They have a calorific value of around 360, with a cooking time of between twelve and fifteen minutes.

Ration Packs

You may wish to choose a ration pack, which contains all your daily food requirements. Most are based on thorough research and give a tasty, nutritious and well-balanced diet. Most ration packs are especially enriched with protein and

minerals and have a high calorie content, designed to provide a high proportion of complex carbohydrates, which provide the body with a form of fuel easily converted into energy.

Ration packs come in lightweight variations for those intending to stay away from civilization for a long time, and also in normal one-, two- and three-day packs. In addition to the main meals, ration packs contain all other sundries needed for eating and cooking outdoors.

Survival Rations

Survival rations are designed to keep you alive and supply you with energy. There are some which are no more than a vitaminized biscuit made from 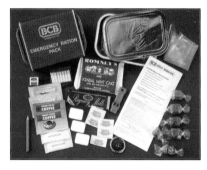 compressed ingredients. You don't want to know about these! They are intended for real long-term survival and should not be purchased for outdoor recreational activities. A better option is to buy a purpose-made survival ration which has the benefit of having been tested over a period of years.

Survival Food

Always remember you are in the mountains to enjoy yourself and not to ravage the countryside. There are many books on survival, all of which demonstrate how to forage for food by putting down traps and picking wild plants. Don't do it. If you have prepared properly, you should have sufficient food and water to last you for at least two days. Even if you have nothing with you, the body can last up to four days without water and four weeks without any food, so there is no justification for using survival food techniques within Europe, other than using a survival ration. For those walking or climbing in the wilderness of America, India or Asia, the problem of survival can be greatly reduced through good planning and communications.

WATER

Nothing is more important to your survival than your water supply. The human body – itself about 70 per cent water – cannot maintain its efficiency without a regular minimum intake. The amount required varies according to climate and the level of activity being carried out. Even in a temperate climate the daily requirement is 2.5 litres (4.5 pints). If your efficiency is to be maintained, this requirement has to be met. In addition, everything possible must be done to make certain that the water is pure. Water procurement involves two factors: quality and quantity

Water Safety

By and large, tapwater is safe enough, as is the water drawn from small streams in uninhabited mountainous areas (although purification is advised for any outdoor water source). It is essential to remember that much surface water, especially if stagnant or muddy, will be contaminated with

waterborne diseases and will be extremely dangerous to drink unless purified. **Do not underestimate this risk.** The disease-inducing and other harmful organisms contained in impure water constitute one of the greatest enemies of survival. If your only source of water is impure – or even suspect – do not drink any until it has been filtered and purified.

Water Hazards

Many diseases are caught through drinking contaminated water. These include dysentery, cholera, typhoid and hepatitis A. Water that is contaminated by sewage or dead animals puts you at a very high risk. Even washing in water can be dangerous, as some waterborne molluscs are infested with parasites.

WATER SAFETY

➤ Never drink from any source unless you are certain it is safe. This includes high mountain catchments.

➤ Never drink directly from lakes, rivers, streams, etc.

➤ Boiled water is the safest form of drinking water. Boil for at least five minutes.

➤ Filter and purify all drinking water not from a safe, recognizable source.

Filtering

Recent years have seen the emergence of a range of new (albeit somewhat expensive) water filters which should satisfy most needs. In general, these have a ceramic filter which removes all suspended matter

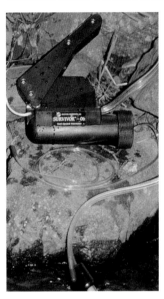

and pathogens, including *E. coli*, cryptosporidium, cholera and amoebae. In most models the filter can be replaced to extend the active life. The units work by placing a tube from the bottom end of the pump into the water and operating a hand pump. A second tube at the top end allows clean water to be collected. Depending on the type you buy, the flow rate to produce one litre (two pints) can vary from one to ten minutes.

It is also worth mentioning that there is now a compact filter which not only removes contamination but also converts seawater into fresh water. This is the smallest hand-operated desalinator in the world, filtering out some 98 per cent of the sea salt.

Purification

The best way to purify water is to treat it with purification tablets, which are available from most chemists and camping outlets. If you prefer you can use effective iodine crystals instead of the tablets. Both crystals and tablets will make contaminated water drinkable in about 15 minutes. The amount of tablets or crystals needed will depend on the type you buy; follow the manufacturer's instructions and never be tempted to add extra as this may cause a build-up of iodine in the body. Remember tablets and crystals only kill the bacteria – they do not filter particles. There is one ingenious device called the water-purifying straw, with which you can suck water directly into your mouth from any source. As the water passes through the straw a remarkable 96 per cent of bacteria and viruses are killed. The straw has a capacity of some 40 litre (70 pints) before the filter becomes waterclogged and ineffective.

Survival Filtering and Purification

You should always choose your water from the freshest source available, the best way being to collect rainwater on a clean plastic sheet. If you cannot do this, a fast-running stream should be used (larger rivers are prone to pollutants from sewage and factories).

The first step towards making water fit to drink is filtration. This will remove any creatures of any size, as well as mud particles, leaves or other foreign matter. Clean sand held in a short sleeve, sock or cloth can be used effectively.

If no purification tablets are available, boil the water for five minutes. Heat the water sufficiently to agitate the water, thereby ensuring equal distribution of heat.

If you are using snow, remember you will use a great deal of fuel to produce a small amount of water. Charcoal bits from your fire, crushed and added an hour before drinking to any purified water, will help remove unpleasant tastes or smells. Don't worry about any small pieces of charcoal left in the water. A small amount will do your stomach more good than harm.

Water Carriers

How much water to carry will depend on the route, and previous experience in the area. Water is heavy, so carry no more than 2 litres (3.5 pints) for a normal walking day where you have breakfasted and dined in accommodation. Where you  intend to camp out overnight, replenish your water as close as possible to your camp site.

There are numerous types of water bottles on the market. For walking, choose one that holds at least 1 litre (2 pints) of water and which will fit neatly into the side pocket of your rucksack. Always check that the top has a good screw-on cap with a waterproof seal. For your base camp you will need a larger container which can be filled locally. This should have a capacity of at least 2 gallons (9 litres).

Winter Mountain Walking

This book is not intended to cover the techniques of ice climbing. However, it would be unwise not to include details of the basic winter walking techniques.

A covering of snow transforms a landscape of mountains, valleys, streams and trees into a marvellous white blanket. Many walkers like the idea of breaking new ground as they walk through a winter landscape, and take great pleasure from the feeling of isolation this gives. However, winter walking also brings with it many dangers which are not present at other times of the year, and a walker should be appropriately prepared.

FITNESS

Winter walking means trudging through sometimes very deep snow for many hours. The effort required and the energy consumed can be up to three times that for normal walking. Extra clothing, food and fuel will have to be carried, thus increasing the weight of your rucksack, and walking into strong winds or snow blizzards will severely reduce the body's ability to function efficiently. All these extra factors mean that a walker should have a very high level of fitness before venturing out in the winter.

PRECAUTIONS

Walking in the mountains, especially in the Scottish Highlands, during winter is a serious business, and one that should be undertaken only by a group of suitably equipped experienced walkers, preferably with a local guide. All precautions should be taken to balance the walkers' requirement for a sense of freedom with the risk to the lives of those who may have to search for and rescue them.

Make sure that you go out properly equipped against the harshest of elements, and that you carry sufficient survival equipment to see you through any emergency. A sensible walker will carefully consider and plan his route across the winter terrain in advance, making sure that the walk can be completed in daylight (a maximum of six hours and often shorter in the Scottish Highlands), leaving a plan of his route with a responsible person. Ridge walking should be avoided whenever possible, especially

where cornices of overhanging snow have formed.
Under no circumstances should you venture close to
edge of a cornice as from above it will be unclear
where the rock ends and the overhang begins. Steep-
sided mountains may well harbour areas of snow-
covered scree, and while the surface may look intact,
underlying rock may well slide away.

FROZEN LAKES AND RIVERS

Frozen lakes and rivers are to be found during any
winter travel and they are all fraught with danger. No
matter how cold the temperature, ice can **never** be
considered safe especially in spring when the shore
line starts to thaw and sheet ice disintegrates into
candle ice. If you must cross ice, check that it is solid
and capable of supporting your weight. Carry a long,
strong pole and hold it with both hands in the centre,
this will provide a bridge and extraction hold should
you fall through the ice. The pole can also be used to
test suspicious patches of ice.

Loosen any rucksack or snowshoe straps, so that they can be easily shaken off should you fall through the ice. Put on extra clothing and wear some form of floatation aid. Stay close to the bank and firm ground, and make sure that any members of your group are tied together at 5 m (15 ft) intervals with each carrying their own safety pole.

Partly frozen rivers and streams can be crossed providing you are aware of the water depth at its lowest point and it is safe to wade across. If you do this, remove your socks (not your boots) and trousers before crossing, using your pole as a staff in the water. Replace your dry socks and trousers once safely across. Your upper clothing should protect your body temperature but be aware that entering ice-cold water can induce momentary paralysis. Swimming in ice-cold water will rapidly reduce your body temperature as any movement produces body heat, which is lost to the surrounding water. Your body temperature is 37°C, when immersed in ice-cold water this will fall by 1°C every two minutes, when your body reaches 33°C you will flounder into unconsciousness and at 25°C you will be dead.

FALLING THROUGH ICE

If you fall through ice it will knock the breath out of you. Stay calm and try to act rationally as continuous hyperventilation can lead to unconsciousness causing you to drown. Try not to swallow cold water as this will make you choke and cool your inner body. You will ball-up with muscle contractions and there is the

danger that younger and older people could die from a heart attack. You must do everything within your power to resurface through the entry hole and pull yourself free. Extend and drop both arms out onto the ice; if it breaks free keep trying until you have a solid purchase. Try orientating yourself towards the direction from which you came, and exit over ice you have walked over. Grip on your pole or use it to lever yourself out. Remain prone at all times even when out of the water; retrace your steps to the shore or riverbank.

If you go under the ice you have little chance of survival but there are several cases where people have come out alive. The best method is to kick at the ice above with your feet until you can make a hole through which to surface, then follow the procedure above.

Rolling in fresh snow will act as a blotter but this is only a temporary reprieve. You need to make a fire and shelter from the wind because without either you will die. If you do not take immediate action, you will start to become unconscious in 5–10 minutes with death following 20 minutes later. Depending on the weather conditions this gives you around 30 minutes to build a fire before your hands, mind and body become immobile.

Take off wet clothing and remove as much water as possible by twisting and squeezing before they freeze. Put on extra clothing and exercise for a few minutes; this can take the form of collecting fuel for a fire if available. If there are several people in the party, share some of your outer clothes temporarily. It is better to be naked for a short while and you will survive longer than staying in wet clothes. Once you have fire and shelter, avoid panic! You must dry and warm you body first before your clothes. Water can be removed from frozen cloths by beating them with a stick. If you manage to survive, then you must rest. Once you have been thoroughly chilled it will take several hours for your body to return to normal, so make sure you are fully recovered before continuing.

SAS ACTION

➤ An SAS soldier would always have his spare clothing and sleeping bag in a waterproof bag inside his rucksack when crossing water, frozen or otherwise. Additionally he would always have the means to light an instant fire packed in a waterproof container before venturing onto the ice.

AVALANCHES

It is almost impossible to predict when an avalanche is

going to occur. Even in Europe, where scientists have studied the phenomenon for years, it is still difficult to forecast a precise time and place. However, slopes which have an angle of between 30° and 45°, and where the depth of snow is more than 30 cm (1 ft), are those which are most at risk from avalanches. It is therefore important to recognize the factors which cause avalanches.

The ground may have been previously covered with a layer of old snow which has deteriorated through fluctuations in temperature to form a smooth, hard, flat surface. A thicker layer of soft snow may well have built up on top of this base. The angle of slope, gravity and the speed and direction of the wind will all contribute to making the top layer of snow move, thus causing an avalanche. This sort of avalanche is know as a soft slab avalanche and is the most common type.

Avalanche Assessment

Knowledge of snowfalls in the previous week, the temperature and the wind strength will all help in an assessment of what lies beneath any fresh snow fall. Asking local guides about high-risk areas and adjusting your route accordingly is also a good idea. Continue to adjust your assessment during your walk, by taking note of how the snow is reacting to your weight on it: is the snow crisp and firm beneath your feet or is it loose and rolling away down the slope? If you see snow breaking up and falling away, even in a small area, you should consider yourself at risk and move if at all possible to level ground.

USING AN ICE AXE

If you are walking during the winter, the chances are that at some point you will have to climb a steep snow-covered slope. An ice axe is therefore an advisable item of equipment to carry. This is a mountaineering tool which has a blade-shaped adze and a curved serrated pick attached to a spiked shaft. Ice axes come in a variety of lengths, but for mountain walking an axe with a handle 70 cm (2 ft) long is recommended. A sling should also be attached to the axe so that it can be put round the wrist and not lost in the event of a fall.

On flat ground an ice axe is best carried attached to the outside of your rucksack or in a holster around the waist. Only when climbing, traversing or descending should the ice axe be used. When in use, the ice axe should be held in the right hand, gripping the head where it meets the shaft, as one would a walking stick.

When walking uphill, the shaft is best

pushed into the snow for support, while you make steps in the snow with your boots. On steeper slopes or while traversing, you may find it easier to use a two-handed grip on the axe.

When descending a steep slope, it is best to face inwards towards the slope, using both hands on the ice axe for support, and making steps with the toes of your boots. On gently-sloping downhill slopes, it is safe to walk forwards, using the axe as a walking stick and by digging in the heels of your boots for support.

If you should fall on a snow-covered slope, use your ice axe to break your slide. There are a number of methods for arresting your fall by using an ice axe, but the following method is safe to use in most situations.

➤ If you feel yourself falling, always try to sit down in the snow, gripping the ice axe head in your left hand and with your right hand firmly on the shaft about half way down.

➤ As you start to slide, dig the point of the shaft into the snow as hard as you can, and hold it there. You may not stop straight away, but the action will certainly arrest your fall.

➤ At the first opportunity, roll off your back and face the snow, at the same time driving the pick head into the snow with as much force as possible. This action should stop your fall.

Remember at all times that ice axes are dangerous tools, and unless they are properly used can cause injury. You should certainly take instruction in the use of an ice axe if you intend to use it for anything more than mountain walking.

WINTER WALKING

- ➤ Check the weather forecast before setting off and constantly be aware of the weather during your walk.
- ➤ Consult a local guide or expert about the route you intend to follow.
- ➤ Plan your route with care and leave a copy of it with a responsible person and have a cut-off time for your return.
- ➤ Do not walk alone.
- ➤ Dress using the layer principle (see p. 45). Salopettes are warmer than trousers for winter walking. Protect your hands and head with thermal gloves, a neck-over and a balaclava.
- ➤ Wear comfortable walking boots which are appropriate for winter use.
- ➤ Wear gaiters to protect your boots and lower legs.
- ➤ Carry an ice axe, but learn how to use it beforehand.
- ➤ The amount of calories in the food you carry should be twice that for a summer walk.
- ➤ Remember to carry a flask of hot soup, as portable cookers do not work well in wintry conditions.
- ➤ Watch where you walk. Keep a lookout for signs of avalanches (see p. 126).
- ➤ If you get into trouble, retrace your steps or walk towards the nearest point of known safety.

Rock Climbing

It is difficult to say where mountain walking ends and rock climbing begins. Mountain walking normally incorporates a route which takes you over mountains and through the valleys. In doing so the most difficult obstacle you should encounter will be a boulder or rocky outcrop that is perfectly safe for you to climb. Rock climbing on the other hand is a totally different

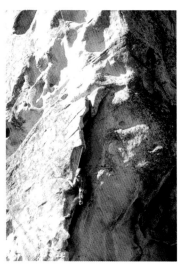

pastime. Most rock climbers will drive and park at the nearest convenient place in respect to the rock face they intend to climb. As with mountain walking routes most rock climbing routes are graphically illustrated and described in a climbing book available for the area. The degree of difficulty varies from climb to climb, thus it is possible for a novice to learn and practise on the less dangerous climbs, while those with more competent skills can try out the harder routes.

Rock climbing is a sports pursuits skill which can be learnt and improved. It can be fun and is certainly challenging.

SAS ACTION

➤ Most of my SAS career was spent as a member of Mountain Troop, a group of approximately 16 men. Mountain Troop is responsible for all aspects of mountaineering and skiing required in order to facilitate military operations. Training for the troop takes several forms. At times the whole troop may embark on a rock-climbing course where new members, with no previous experience, will be taught the basics of rock climbing and abseiling techniques. Depending on length of service and aptitude, many individuals will attended courses in Europe, with a selected few attending the German Alpine Guides course. This is held at the German Mountain Warfare school in Mitten-wald and normally lasts a year, with the Germans allowing two SAS personnel per course. The Mountain Guides course is divided into summer and winter mountain skills, and those that qualify return both expert climbers and skiers. The SAS also run their own Alpine training course and several SAS members have climbed Everest.

TYPES OF CLIMBING

Over the years climbing has changed and expanded, especially with the growth of sports climbing. Additionally, safety, which is the backbone of all climbing, has been dramatically improved with the invention of new climbing aids and techniques. Today, climbing can be divided into four areas, traditional, sports, big rock and ice.

AUTHOR'S NOTE

➤ This book offers a general guide to traditional climbing techniques intended only to illustrate the procedures and usages of the equipment required. Ice and sports climbing are briefly mentioned for interest and to highlight the differences.

Traditional

This is the way most people learn to climb. It involves learning the art of finding a route up a rock face and climbing up it. As rock is a natural element no two routes are the same, however, many share the same attributes in as much as they all are steep, are covered with cracks, ledges, holes and rough surfaces. Climbers use their hands, feet and body by holding or griping. To aid safety they are attached to a rope which is fixed either to a strong point (belay) at either the top or the bottom of the route. For safety along the route they can attach a number of different devices (protection) which should stop them falling to their death. Traditional climbing is normally done with two or three people working together, with the most experienced climber taking the lead. The routes vary in length, some can be climbed in a single pitch while others are divided into several pitches.

Sports Climbing

On the surface you could argue that there is little difference between traditional climbing and sports climbing, but you would be wrong. Traditional

climbing means that the lead climber will ascend a route placing his protection as and when possible or required. When confronted with a difficult piece of rock they will endeavour not to fall. By contrast the sports climber will climb on a route where the protection is fixed having only to hang in a quickdraw and snap in the rope. All their stamina and physical ability will be focused not on the protection but on completing the move. Where a traditional climber will do all in his power to prevent a fall, sports climbers get used to falling with regular frequency. Few climbers have the skill and confidence to place good removable protection while suspended upside down under a fifteen foot overhand hundreds of feet over the deck. The freedom of sports climbing challenges the climbers full physical potential under fairly safe conditions and is what makes this form of climbing so addictive.

Sports climbing also requires less gear, making it cheaper than traditional climbing. The sports routes are often easier to access and when they are not, indoor rock gyms offer excellent facilities on which to learn and compete.

Big Rock or Alpine Climbing

While the basic techniques are similar to those of traditional climbing there is a vast difference in the scale of the rock climbed. Big rock and Alpine climbing requires multi-pitch techniques which in some cases can take several days or longer to complete. Both the duration on the rock and the height put extra strain on the climbers. Extra protection is required, plus equipment specially designed for sloping overnight belayed to the rock face. Many of the height climbs also require the use of ice climbing gear, and environmental protection. While countless climbers challenge the big rocks for pleasure, to a large extent big rock and Alpine climbing is a prelude to a more serious mountainous expedition such as Mount Everest.

Ice Climbing

Ice climbing differs from all over forms of climbing. Although you still climb using your hands and feet, the tactile feeling of safety you get from actually touching the rock is anaesthetised by the use of ice axes and crampons. While protection has been developed to deal with the problems of climbing ice, the ice itself can vary so much that it renders

protection useless. Have no doubts falling on ice carries much stiffer penalties. It is not a sport for the weak and pain from one source or another go hand in hand with ice climbing.

Those that insist on proving their manhood/ womanhood will also need to take out a small bank loan to cover the cost of equipment. If you try to ice climb on the cheap, you may as well make your own funeral arrangements beforehand. You will need boots, both leather for hard, warm-conditions climbing and plastic for cold conditions. Your body requires layered and outer shell clothing to protect you from the cold and that is just for starters. You will also require, ropes, gloves and mittens, crampons, ices pitons and chemical heat packs to unfreeze your fingers. Then there are the touring skis or shoes which make it possible for you to reach the base of the climb.

AUTHOR'S NOTE

➤ My first experience at ice climbing was on the Aiguille du Midi above Chamonix, in France, and despite being summer it was not a pleasant experience. I was tooled-up and told to traverse what looked like a solid sheet of ice. I say looked like because although smooth the surface was extremely wet, with tiny rivulets dribbling down into a large hole which resembled a mouth in the glacier – one slip and you would never be seen again. I did as instructed, driving the tips of my crampons into the ice with every functioning leg muscle, while hammering home the ice axes. To the delight of my French instructor, I completed the traverse back onto firm ground with no problem, but had they asked me to do it again, I think I would have chickened out. It's not that I am a coward, it's just that some risks hold no pleasure.

You may consider yourself a good climber, but ice is totally different. If you are stuck on giving it a try, then I suggest you seek out professional guidance and training. To get the feel of working on ice start by doing a few short routes using a top rope. This will get you used to the equipment and give you a feel for climbing with crampons and ice axe techniques. When you feel confident enough to lead, start on something very, short and very safe. Unlike rock ice changes with age, weather and temperature, it can be hard, flaky, soft and watery. Furthermore ice climbing is just the start of the problem, venturing into snow-covered areas means brushing up on your winter survival, first-aid and rescue skills.

WARNING

➤ Never be tempted to rush off and climb alone. It's the easiest way to end up dead. While sports climbing can be learnt on an individual basis through various tuition courses using an indoor climbing gym, I personally believe you are better off learning to climb in the outdoor traditional way first.

LEARNING TO CLIMB

No matter what type of climbing you want to do you have to start at the beginning. Neither this book nor any other DIY climbing book will help you become a good climber; if you want to climb you have to go out and do it for real. It takes many years of practise to perfect rock-climbing skills and the only way to learn is to undergo proper rock-climbing instruction. Join a club or attend a climbing school.

If there is no club or school near you then you may be lucky enough to find a qualified climber living nearby who is willing to teach you. The essence of traditional climbing is being in control, which means having confidence in you protection. Finding the right spot on the rock and attaching the correct protection is the only skill that really matters.

CLIMBING FITNESS

Climbing is a strenuous and exacting activity no matter what form it takes. It is therefore obvious that anyone who participates in such an activity should be fit. Most rock-climbing routes are fairly inaccessible and require a long uphill walk carrying all your equipment. You will need good cardiovascular capacity, coupled with muscle strength and stamina, and a great degree of flexibility. Mountain walking is one way of building up the right muscles, and you will always find large boulders suitable for a hands-and-feet technique work-out. These boulders should be large enough for you to climb making several hand holds on before reaching the top, yet not so high that if you fall you will hurt yourself. Bouldering is a well-practised technique used by climbers who wish to improve their grip, reach and associated skills.

Training in a rock gym may make you competent at climbing quickly and there is no doubt that it will vastly improve your strength, style and ability. However, there will be a distinct skills gap when you climb outdoors, because a rock gym cannot replicate the wind, rain, temperature and differing rock structures of the real thing, and these will search out your weaknesses. In addition, I have discovered that confidence gained from the high degree of protection offered in most rock gyms does not relate to that required when converted to traditional climbing.

EQUIPMENT

Today many climbers start their passage to rock climbing in the gym. This is a good idea as the equipment you need to buy is minimal. In addition it helps you get a feel for the sport while building up the required muscles. However, as you progress to the real thing you will find a great difference and you will require a lot more equipment. By and large it is true to say that the longer and harder the climbing route the more tools you will need, and this can become an ongoing drain on your financial resources. So if you are considering climbing, buy equipment that will last.

Your first visit to a climbing store is akin to entering Aladdin's cave, its full of wonderful brightly coloured ropes, slings and metal gadgets. If you're starting from scratch, the first thing you need is your personal gear: shoes, helmet, chalk bag, harness, rope, karabiners, plus a few other nuts and bolts. My advice would be to forget about the more complicated hardware, such as expensive camming devices, until you have learnt a little bit more about actual climbing. By and large the owners of most climbing stores have been climbers themselves, so ask for and consider their advice. If they try to offload you with some mysterious, unrecognisable item, decline it. For example, it is obvious that rock climbing requires a purpose-made shoe or boot, a helmet will protect your head and harness will hold all your equipment. Likewise, who has ever seen a rock climber without a rope? Well there are many that 'free climb' but we will not go into that in this book. What you are doing is buying a protection system, as almost every piece of climbing equipment is designed not to make the climb easier but to afford you protection where the climb may be difficult.

Shoes and Boots

Never buy shoes via mail order, go to a shop with a large selection and preferably one which has a climbing wall. Start off with a firm-fitting yet comfortable pair of all-round climbing shoes/boots.

Helmet

Choose a helmet that is approved by and conforms to the safety standards required by the sport.

Harness

There are many forms of climbing harness on the market and I would advise you to chose one that will meet your needs for several years. Check that the harness is large enough to fit over the thickest clothing. Avoid lightweight sport harnesses, or those that will encumber you when your halfway

up a chimney crack. Check the webbing because you'll want waist loops for racking gear. My personal recommendation for traditional climbing would be something like the Petzl 'Falcon' Harness. This is heavy duty, well padded, easily adjustable and comes with a D-ring attachment.

Rope

Ropes are used in climbing as a means of safety while climbing or descending a steep rock face. There are several types of rope used, but the most common is nylon. A rope should have a certain amount of elasticity, providing a low impact on the climber should they fall and be arrested by it. By comparison ropes used for abseiling should have a minimum of elasticity. Most beginners ought to choose a medium type 11 mm rope which can be used for both climbing and abseiling. This is less likely to wear out and will survive better when rubbed against sharp rock edges. Ropes do get wet so choose one that is water-resistant treated. The rope should also be long enough to complete the whole climb or each main belay section of the climb. A 200-foot (60-m) length should happily satisfy most pitches a beginner will encounter. Once you have selected you rope your should treat it with care

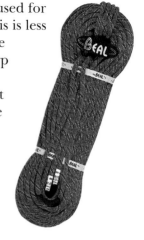

ROPE CARE

➤ Always inspect ropes prior to usage; check for cuts, abrasions, fraying, worn spots and mildew.

➤ Hang a wet rope in a warm room to dry; never dry by applying direct heat.

➤ Avoid running ropes over sharp rocks or ledges.

➤ Never step on a rope or leave it lying in the mud.

➤ Avoid crossing ropes as nylon to nylon friction will harm the ropes.

➤ Avoid contamination from oils, acids, etc.

➤ Wash in clean water, coil loosely and dry in a warm (not direct sunlight) place.

Slings

Flat nylon webbing is used by climbers
for a variety of reasons the main one
being slings. The webbing is available
in flat or tubular tape and comes in a
wide range of sizes and colours. The
type and thickness of the webbing will
depend on the task you wish it to
perform. The webbing is usually
bought from a continuous role
and cut to size using a hot knife or
scissors in order to prevent the
ends fraying. The maintenance
rules for webbing are basically the same
as those for ropes.

Slings are basic climbing items, but make no mistake
they are one of the best aids you can carry. The
heavier webbing can be used to facilitate a belay
point, and there is nothing so solid as a runner
around a chockstone. They can be slipped into flaky
rock or placed on a rock horn, where the flat surface
of the webbing will give better purchase than a round
rope.

Rocks and Nuts

Rocks and Nuts are angular metal devices used primarily
for safety. Their different shapes and sizes are so designed
to allow them to fit into rock cracks and crevices and on
the whole, they are easier and quicker to fit than pitons.
Some, especially the smaller ones, have a wire loop
attached while others are drilled to take a webbing loop.

In general, rocks and nuts are used for extra safety. The climber chooses the correct sized chock for the available crack and inserts it so that at least two sides of the device are wedged into the wall. Once securely fitted into the crack, the device supplies one-direction resistance depending on the wedge angle. Always check that the device is securely in place by wriggling and pulling at it. Once satisfied, you can attach the rope with the use of a karabiner. To release the chock push it back so the wedged sides become free. Rocks and nuts that have become stuck can be tapped out with a piton and hammer.

Use wire nuts for the smaller cracks but make sure the rock is solid; hard sandstone and quartz will take the smallest of wedges. Use a larger device where the rock is softer looking for passive placements first, keeping your cams (see below)for places where rocks and nuts don't work. Always test your protection by giving it a good pull; this also help seat the device more securely in the crack. When selecting passive protection, choose a nut that conforms to the crack and touches as much as possible of the rock surface.

Cams

I was rather intrigued when I saw my first spring-loaded camming device. It looked more like

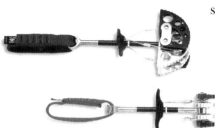

something a garage mechanic should be using rather than a device for climbing. Since then cams have come on in leaps and bounds and now offer some of the best protection you can buy because they work in places where nothing else will, added to which they are quick. However, that said, I have always placed my cams with due care, taking note of the anticipated direction of pull.

Pitons

Like the rest of your climbing gear pitons come in all shapes and sizes, to fit the smallest hairline crack to something over 15 cm (6 inches) in width. Some are rigid or made of hard steel while others are soft and pliable, so that they will bend and conform as they are hammered into the rock. Most modern pitons are made of chrome molybdenum hard steel and are classified into three main groups: blades, angles and leepers.

The normal flat **blade pitons** are used for the smaller cracks and are driven into a suitable fissure with the eye downwards in horizontal cracks.

Make sure the piton is set firmly into the roc

Angles have a V- or U-shaped configuration and are placed in a similar way to flat blade pitons.

Leepers have a Z-shaped configuration and are used in larger cracks. They are placed with the eye uppermost in vertical cracks and downwards in horizontal cracks.

Gravity is what pulls us down when we fall, therefore it make sense that a piton placed in a horizontal crack has a better mechanical advantage than one placed in a vertical crack. Those horizontal cracks which slope down into the rock offer the best security for placing a piton. Evaluate the crack before selecting the appropriate piton, which should easily penetrate the crack for two-thirds of its length before you need to hammer. Do not overdrive the piton, the resistance to your hammering should indicate when to stop. Ideally, the piton should penetrate firmly with just the eye showing. If the piton is firmly placed but not seated to its full length, tie off a sling in a clove hitch. Pitons should only be used as a last resort, and only when chocks and camming do not work. Always try to avoid damaging the rock when placing or removing a piton.

Karabiners or Snap links

The difference between a karabiner and a snap link is purely down to the part of the world in which you are climbing, because in reality they one and the same. Karabiners are metal joints which are used to attach ropes and slings to key points while climbing or

abseiling. These key points can be the climber's body, a top or bottom belay point or an intermediate safety point on the climbing route. Karabiners can be made from steel, aluminium, or various metal alloys and come in many shapes, the most common being oval. Most have a spring gate which when pressed opens allowing the rope to enter. These gates can be either locking or non-locking. The most important feature of a karabiner is its strength and most have the breaking strain stamped into the metal. When strain is placed on a karabiner the weakest parts are the gate pin and locking eye. The strength of the eye can be improved by choosing a karabiner with a screw gate. This is a simple thread which when twisted rides up to cover the locking eye, which not only strengthens the joint but stops the gate from accidentally opening when in use.

KARABINER CARE

Always check the following:

➤   Check for rope wear, chips, cracks and similar damage.
➤   Check that the gate spring is not damaged or too stiff.
➤   Check that the thread on any screw-gate karabiners is clean and free-running.

Quickdraws

Quickdraws are basically two karabiners connected by a webbing strap. They are especially good where you are required to place protection in a precarious potion because they are quick and simple.

TRADITIONAL CLIMBING TECHNIQUES

Traditional climbing involves one or more climbers usually possessing varying degrees of expertise. The most experienced member of the party will be proclaimed the leader who will lead the others up the rock. Those leading do so while secured by a rope to a bottom belay point. Added protection is fixed as they climb until they reach the top belay point where they will secure the rope and instruct those behind to climb up. The last one up will remove the bottom belay and remove the protection devices as he encounters them.

BASIC CLIMBING RULES 1

➤ Avoid any loose rock when climbing and always make sure that you have three points of contact.

➤ Always make sure that it is possible to climb back down again if you need to.

➤ Stay out of snow fields, glaciers and overhanging snow.

Keeping in Contact with the Rock

As previously mentioned we climb with our hands and

feet utilising the cracks and fissures in the rock face in order to get grip and purchase. It makes sense that the more points of contact you have with the rock the safer you should be. Luckily, man can climb using just one point of contact at a time leaving three in place, therefore three points of contact should be maintained whenever possible. The way we grip the rock will depend on the size, shape and depth of the crack or purchase. For example a vertical crack may be wide enough to take all four fingers up to the second knuckle (a good hold); by contrast your foot may be balanced on a toe hold that is nothing more than a minute protrusion on the rock face (not a good hold).

Jamming

In addition to griping the rock with four fingers and standing on a nice little shelf which accommodates the whole foot, there are several techniques you can develop for when the hand and foot holds become scarce or minuscule. This is known as 'jamming', but a wide variety of names have been derived depending on how the hand or foot is used. No matter what you call it, jamming hurts and it's unnatural. Your fingers and hands were never designed to be forced into some small rock crevice where they would support the bulk of your body weight. However, you do need to develop a few basic holds. I found the best way to do this was to look for a small face no more than 3 m (10 ft) high that offered lots of variation for hand and foot grips. You should then practise a variety of finger jams using just the tips right through to a balled fist. If you can't get a good grip, try a twisting action or experiment until you find something that works. It will prove painful, often involving the loss of some skin, but you will be amazed at what can be achieved with a little practise.

Cracks

I mentioned that we climb safely by moving one limb at a time with the other three placed as firmly as possible on the rock. The hands normally lead, but where the hands go the feet must follow, so always take a good look at what you will be forcing your foot onto or into, because this will give you some idea of correct foot position. If the crack is thin, try dropping your knee to the outside while inserting the tip of your shoe sideways into the crack. If the crack offers little more than the bear minimum of support, that is, you have little more than a friction hold, try to make sure the other two points of contact are extremely good before contemplating your next move. Where the

crack is large enough to take several centimetres of your toe you should consider this a good hold, however, beware of jamming your foot in too tightly. When the crack is really wide you can get a firmer grip by using your heel and toe. Strangely, I always found foot jamming more tiring than using my hands.

Offwidths

Where the cracks are really big (sometimes referred to as 'offwidths' – don't ask me why) you will be able

to use your limbs and body. You do this by inserting your arm or leg deep into the crack and searching for some purchase. Where none is found you revert to fist and foot jamming. You do this in such a manner that your outer hands are spread out over the rock face as if you where gripping the corner of a building. Big cracks are usually quite long and you progress up them by levering yourself up by jamming and pushing with your feet.

Chimneys

Cracks large enough to climb into are referred to as chimneys. By and large, providing the chimney is not too wide, climbing these can be fairly easy and relatively safe. There are several ways of

How to climb a chimney: the best way is to use your hands back and your feet pressed against the opposing wall. Draw your legs up and then straighten them.

climbing a chimney, the most common being to press your back and hands against one wall with your feet on the other. Flex your knees or extend your toes to increase the resistance. Another way is to scissor your hands and feet against the opposing walls. In many cases you may decide to use a variety of different manoeuvres in order to climb the chimney. Although chimneys are easy and fairly safe to climb you should be aware that in the majority of cases they offer little in the way of protection.

Other Hand and Foot Techniques

The other hand and foot techniques you are likely to come across will include laybacks, mantelshelf and undercut handholds. These are relatively straightforward and samples are shown below.

Finger tip hold

Four finger hold

Double hand hold

Toe hold

Foot hold

Layback

ROUTE-FINDING

In the traditional world of rock climbing route finding refers to the actual route up or across the rock face. These are rarely in straight lines, instead they wander upwards following a crab-like motion following the best hand and foot holds. On the more recognised routes these holds are easy to see due to the usage of previous climbers. Those that are not so obvious can be followed from the details given in a route guide. Before starting an unknown route always check it out from the ground first. If you have a route guide, confirm the prominent features because this will normally indicate the line you must follow. Unless you are fully qualified or have taken the precaution of climbing on a top rope belay, never chance climbing an unknown route. What may start of as an easy climb could end up with you running out of places to go, forcing you to consider a dangerous retreat.

Most of the loose rock will have been removed on the popular routes but even rock suffers from wear and tear. If you accidentally dislodge a piece of rock make, sure you call out to those beneath you – 'Below!' is the most accepted call. Always test hand and foot holds for any loose rock and work your way around them if at all possible.

Once the lead climber has gone a few metres it is normal to start fixing some form of protection. It should be noted that although tied to a rope the lead climber has no safeguard against falling until the first protection is put in place. This protection comes in a variety of shapes and devices but all share the same common function; they are inserted into the rock surface and have a karabiner attached. The rope that is secured to both the climber and the bottom belay point runs through this karabiner. In the event that the lead climber should fall the weight is taken by the man operating the bottom belay point. This form of protection is mainly reliant on the correct placement of the device, and the more protective devices used the greater the safety factor.

Traditional climbers communicate through a series of calls which also aid climbing safety.

CLIMBING CALLS

➤ 'That's me.' From the climber, this will indicate to the belay that he is ready to climb.

➤ 'Climb when your ready.' Is the usual acknowledgement from the belay.

➤ 'Climbing now.' From the climber.

➤ 'Tight Rope.' Used by the climber to indicate that they are about to make a precarious move and or position.

➤ 'Take in the slack.' Means take in any slack rope.

➤ 'Aye, Aye.' Compliance to any request.

Beginners will find themselves learning to climb on a route that is no higher than a single rope length. However, as you progress you will learn how to handle multi-pitch routes. This simply means that the route you are climbing will need to be completed in several pitches. For example, if two people are climbing then

the lead climber will climb to the first pitch and establish a belay on which he will bring the second man up. From this point the lead climber will continue his assent to the top of the next pitch and so on until both have reached the summit. While this sounds relatively easy, some of the longer rock climbs, especially those of America, require careful planning. You need to know how long the route is going to take to climb because the last thing you want to do is get stuck on the rock face in fading light. Swiftness is safety in multi-pitch climbing, but this should come from competence, not rushing. Keep up your momentum when climbing, only resting when on the belay stances. Some of the midway belay stances can offer an extremely tight fit even for one person.

You will require extra ropes and equipment, and on longer routes you may even need food and water not to mention wet-weather clothing. Leaders and seconds may decide to climb while carrying spare equipment in a rucksack, otherwise you will need to haul your equipment up as your ascend. Hauling can be strenuous and will cost you time, in addition haul lines have a tendency to snarl. Once the first belay stance has been reached, use a 9 mm line to haul in the bag. Take care that neither the bag nor the rope catch on loose rocks, causing them to fall on your second below. Make sure you clip the bag to the belay before you bring your partner up. If the bag gets seriously stuck, the second will have to free it as he climbs. Depending on the climb, you might decide to haul some pitches and carry rucksacks on others.

BASIC CLIMBING RULES 2

➤ Whenever you climb, climb safely.
➤ Protect the mountains.
➤ If camping, avoid destroying delicate plant life.
➤ Strip and pack out old slings.
➤ Don't 'clean' alpine vegetation from cracks on route.
➤ Respect cliff-dwelling birds.
➤ Chalk lightly.

PROTECTION

As I stated at the beginning of this section, protection is the one skill you must master. It is what makes rock climbing possible (yes, I know there are those who free climb, but their first fall is their last). Your confidence in your protection placement ability should reflect in the fact that even if you did fall you would be safe. In order to achieve this you must understand the various types of rock structure and the features they offer which allow you to place protection. Always study the rock, run you hand over it, look what is happening to it. Does it support vegetation? Is it crumbling? Is moisture being extruded? Search out the rock's hidden secrets, look for the cracks both horizontal and vertical, feel for pockets, horns and knobs. Assimilate all this information and choose the appropriate protection, keeping in mind that you should place the simplest device that works. As a beginner, spend time on the ground using a boulder to check out what works best and where, place the protection high enough for you to swing on it and test its strength. Take time to study what others are doing, and ask questions – traditional climbers take pride in placing their protection and will be happy to advise.

Never trust your life to one piece of protection, always back it up. Your climb is not finished until you have returned to the ground. If you are walking off, always check well ahead to make sure it is safe to climb down. Never top rope or rappel on a single piece of protection even if this means leaving equipment behind. Before you climb or descend check everything, and when you climb protect yourself.

Belaying

Belaying is every climber's most crucial form of protection. It means that one person is climbing on the end of a rope while another is securely fixed to some solid protection. By such means if any climber should fall the belayer and the belay will hold them.

*Belaying: make sure you are securely tied to the climber (pic. 1)
and feed the rope to accomodate the climber's safety (pic. 2)*

Traditional climbing normally requires both lead and
top rope belaying techniques. The main points on any
belay are:

➤ The anchor is the strongest point available
offering solid protection, this can be either the
rock itself or some form of climbing device.

➤ The attachment between belayer and anchor
which prevents the belayer from being pulled off
the stance.

➤ The belayer is the climber responsible for
constructing the belay and bringing the climber.

➤ The stance is where the belayer sits or stands in
order to bring up the next climber.

➤ The rope is what links the belayer and the
climber.

➤ The climber.

Roping-up

The decision to rope-up will depend on various
factors, the main one being security. You must
consider the ability of those in your climbing party,
taking into account the most inexperienced member.

The degree of difficulty of the rock to be climbed or crossed also needs consideration, as does such factors as exposure and the speed required to safely manoeuvre a pitch. Thus if you need to rope-up, you need to belay.

While belaying provides your security while climbing, you should remember that the belay is only as good as the anchor. It is essential that you select the most solid anchor available, although this is not the only consideration. You must think about the direction of pull, i.e. if the climber falls, will the pull be downwards, upwards or possibly cause a pendulum effec? The belay has to hold both the belayer in the correct position as well as anticipating any fall by the climber.

Thread belay

Spike belay

The best anchor is one that can be pulled in any direction, such as round a tree or a solid rock thread. While such anchors can generally be found at the start and finish of a climb, on multi-pitch routes, you may be forced to use a piton or some other device on the midway belay points. In an ideal situation the anchor should be around head height and close enough to hold the belayer in the correct stance when the rope is under pressure.

AUTHOR'S NOTE

➤ While it is was common practice for the belayer to tie themselves to the same rope in between anchor and climber many climbers now prefer to use a belay plate. The belayer while being attached to the anchor did not run the climbing rope over their shoulder or around their waist. Instead they would use a device with which they could pull the climbing rope through as the climber ascended. In the event of a fall the grip on the rope was enough to hold the climber and allowed the belayer to slip in a securing loop and then assist or advise the climber. If a climber falls when the rope is around the belayer's waist or shoulders, the pressure is immense and the belayer can do little more than hang onto the weight.

The optimum stance is making the best of what is available. You should be in a position where you can follow the climber's progress in order to advise. This is particularly important when climbing with a novice. Position the rope so that it does not run over any sharp edges, or dislodge loose rock. Depending on the anchor height, you should adopt the most comfortable position, generally sitting or standing, which is nearest to the vertical plane between climber and anchor. When the rope comes under tension if there is a fall, and unless otherwise belayed, you will be pulled sideways into this plane.

The belayer should make sure they are secured to the anchor in such a way as to allow them comfortable movement within the stance while avoiding too much slack. If the rope between the anchor and belayer is too slack, there is a chance of being pulled over in the event of the climber falling.

Rope line and Protection

There are several dangers when you start a climb. At the outset you are never safe until you place your first piece of protection. When you leave the ground the rope will run from belayer to the rock, through the first piece of protection and then up to the lead climber, usually creating a bend in the rope. This bend can cause an outward force on your first protection and if its not properly seated it can lift it out. The initial protection has to hold in order to prevent a zipper-type action stripping away all your protection, unlikely but it has happened. To prevent this make sure your first protection device is rock solid or use a multi-directional cam. After the first piece your placement of protection should take into account the rope's path which should be fluid. Try to avoid zigzagging or dragging the rope over sharp edges. Even if protection is not required you may deem it necessary to place a device in order to facilitate the ropes smooth path. Likewise, if the only available protection is off line, consider extending your runners. Always make sure your rope is free-running before attempting to negotiate a hard or difficult move.

KNOTS

There are estimated to be around 3,500 different knots and their variations, and it would take far more space than we have here to describe them all. For the benefit of traditional climbing we need only concentrate on a few, although as your climbing improves you will learn many more. Knots are what secure your rope and runners, and they must work.

AUTHOR'S NOTE

➤ By and large, most knots have the same name but there are variations depending on the language.

Figure-Eight Loop

The basic all-situations knot normally used as your end tie-in knot. The same knot can be interwoven around an object such as a rock or tree.

Double Fisherman's

The best knot for tying two ropes together. Always leave at least a 15-cm (6-inch) tail.

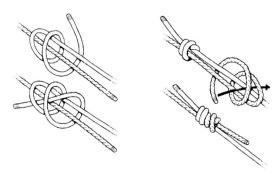

Bowline

An old but reliable knot which can still be used for tying on. Make the loop large enough so that it rides up around the lower part of the ribcage.

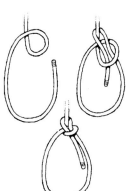

Leave enough tail to tie a overhand knot.
Variations such as a triple bowline and a bowline on the blight are also worth learning at a later date.

Tape Knot

This is used to tie webbing when making slings and runners.

Prusik Knot

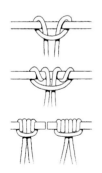

A very useful knot when ascending. It functions very much like a Jumar  in as much that it grips the rope when under tension but will slide when the tension is released.

CLIMBING GRADES

Over the years climbs have been graded depending on their degree of difficultly and the amount of protection it is possible to establish on the route.

Grading is based on the average adult, although it is recognised that certain people may have an advantage or disadvantage while climbing some rock feature. For example, a small woman climber may be able to slip her hand into the smallest of cracks and take purchase, by contrast a tall man may have the reach required to make a move not possible for someone shorter. Grading is something you learn as your climbing skills advance, but they are important because they give a clear indication of the problems you might encounter on a route. Most rock-climbing guide books give a clear indication as to the grade of each climb.

The two-part British system gives the single-move difficulty (4a, 5c, etc.) and an overall grade that accounts for sustained climbing and protection difficulties.

BRITISH CLIMBING GRADES

➤ **S** Severe
➤ **VS** Very severe
➤ **HVS** Hhard very severe
➤ **XS** or **E** Extremely severe (E grades extending from E1 to E9)

In North America the difficulty grades are a modified version of the original Yosemite Decimal System (YDS). There is also a Roman numeral system for the duration of the climb.

> ## US CLIMBING GRADES

➤ **Class 1** Hiking

➤ **Class 1 & 2** Scrambling

➤ **Class 3 & 4** Technical free climbing.

➤ **Class 5 & 6** Aided climbing. (the latter are subdivided to express degrees of difficulty i.e. 5.9 5.11 etc).

DESCENDING

Even before you start climbing you should consider how you are going to get down once you have reached the top. For most beginners this will not pose much of a problem as it will mean moving back from the rock face and finding a scramble route down through the vegetation. As you progress the routes you climb will become longer and there is no guarantee that you will be able to walk about the rock face buttress. Even if there is a walk-off route it may be hazardous. Before you climb, consult your route guide and take time to view the rock wall and its surroundings from a low vantage point. Its no good waiting until you have reached the top and look down, because most of the hazards will be hidden from view.

The roof of a rock-climbing buttress may look flat from the ground but you should take into consideration features such as gullies and scree. The sides of any buttress are generally scattered with large boulders and loose rock, some of which are easily dislodged. The best way to walk down is over ground covered with rough vegetation, facing downwards as you descend. Place your heels in well and grip with the palms of your hands when crossing large boulders. If the going gets steeper, turn sideways and start gripping the rock. Never venture further than you can see.

Abseiling

Having abseiled down rock faces, buildings and from helicopters I have two points to offer. Make sure you are secured to the best belay possible and that the rope is both long enough and strong enough. Moreover, make sure you are correctly secured to the abseil rope and can descend under control. The rest is down to individual technique.

Although you can double the rope around a good belay and lower yourself with the rope over your shoulder and around you waist, I do not recommend

it. Rope friction over the body is not smooth, added to which if you get in trouble there is little you can do to help yourself short of climbing down the rope.

I was taught to abseil with a figure-of-eight device, often referred to in the SAS as the bottle opener. This descender works smoothly, is easy to use and offers a good degree of control. You can stop and tie-off at any point on the descent, allowing you to use both your hands. It is also possible to control the descent by having a person on the ground put tension on the rope. While there are several good descenders on the market, you would be well advised to use the figure of eight.

Once you have checked your belay and attached yourself to the rope you should make your way to the rock lip. By far the most fear-provoking part of abseiling is leaning backwards over the rock face, and there is a tendency to bend the knees and ball-up the body. What is required is that you lean out from the rock wall with your feet wide apart one foot lower than the other with the knees only slightly bent. This will provide stability as you take your first step over the top. Once you are leaning out with your feet firmly on the rock wall simply walk down. There is a tendency for people to let the rope slip through their hands causing a rapid descent. This is fine for the military, or where speed is required in an emergency, but not for normal rock climbing. Always descend under control and at a speed similar to that of a brisk walking pace.

Wilderness First Aid

Walking or climbing in the mountains at any time of year is a serious business, and one that should only be undertaken by qualified people, preferably with a local guide. All precautions should be taken to balance the freedom you desire against the lives of others who may be required to search for, and rescue you.

Make sure that you go out properly equipped against the harshest of elements, and that you carry sufficient equipment to see you through any emergency. The sensible mountain walker or climber will carefully consider their plan making sure it can be completed during the hours of daylight. It is also a good idea to leave a plan of your intended route with a responsible person with cut-off times that indicate an emergency. In general the higher you climb the higher the higher the risk of accident or injury. Whether alone or in a group you should walk at a leisurely pace minimising physical effort. Walking too fast, lifting the legs over rocky or steep ground all put strain on the muscles and joints causing tiredness and aches. Arms and hands should be kept free, so that in the event of a slip or fall they can be used to fend off serious injury. Take extra care when climbing or descending steep slopes, and avoid scree areas. Jumping over rocky terrain or running fast downhill is the easiest way to cause an injury. If any form of serious rock climbing is required, the climber must be qualified enough to tackle the degree of severity that the rock face presents (see Traditional Rock Climbing p. 133).

If you are planning to walk through mountainous areas preparation is essential. Even on a fine summer day, the weather can change rapidly and mist or fog can reduce visibility to just a few metres. It is easy to underestimate how difficult a walk in a mountainous area might be, or how dangerous rocky ground can be. If you do get into difficulties or injure yourself, it may be some time before you can raise the alarm and the emergency services can reach you. You may be adequately dressed, have the proper footwear, and a rucksack full of camping equipment, but this will mean little if you fall and injure yourself. Lying unconscious in the cold and wet leaves little time for a search party to realise you are missing and then find you – hypothermia kills very quickly. Likewise, some injuries, such as uncontrolled bleeding, can also be life threatening.

FIRST-AID KIT

There are many first-aid packs on the market, most of which contain a few plasters and the odd bandage. However, there is one first-aid pack which has been specifically designed for the outdoor enthusiast – the

AUTHOR'S NOTE

➤ The scope of this book is neccessarily limited and the procedures described in this section are designed to cover those injuries and accidents most associated with the mountains. You may wish to obtain more information and practical advice from a local branch of the Ambulance Association, Red Cross or similar organisations. You may also wish to read **Emergency Medic** from the SAS Active Library Series which is designed for wilderness emergencies.

Gregson Lifesaver System. The Gregson pack has been designed to help perform first-aid procedures as you read aloud the instructions, which saves vital seconds. The instructions are easy to follow and the contents easy to find, covering all eventualities from blisters to bleeding, fractures to burns, and even rescue.

If you prefer to assemble your own personal medical first-aid kit, consider what items you will include. The range of survival equipment is vast, with new items coming onto the market every year. However, there are several vital questions you should ask yourself about each item. Is it really necessary? Is its function duplicated by any other item? Are you capable of using the item? Remember, the aim is to keep the kit as small as possible. Once selected, assemble all the pieces of equipment you intend to carry and make sure they are well packed in a totally waterproof container. The simplest way of ensuring the latter is to seal the whole kit in an airtight, plastic, snap-seal food container. Once packed and closed, the container should be sealed with adhesive polythene tape.The items chosen for the kit should reflect your first-aid skill and should include the basic items listed below.

FIRST AID KIT

➤ **Plasters.** A good selection of assorted plasters, but err on the large size, as they can be cut down as required. Use the waterproof type.

➤ **Suture plasters**. A strip of butterfly sutures is ideal for closing small wounds.

➤ **Needles and safety pins.** Various sizes.

➤ **Medical wipes.** Two strips.

➤ **Paraffin burn dressing.**

➤ **Large wound dressings.** Always carry at least one large wound dressing.

(contd)

➤ **Aspirin.** At least two dozen soluble aspirins to relieve mild pain and headaches. They can also reduce fever.

➤ **Diarrhoea powder and rehydration mix.**

➤ **Antihistamine cream.** Insect bites and stings can cause severe irritation.

➤ **All-purpose antiseptic cream.**

➤ **Water purification tablets.** You will need two dozen.

➤ **Small pair of scissors.**

➤ **Salt.** A small container of salt should be carried if the climate is very hot.

➤ **A small first-aid book.** Emergency Medic is ideal, in terms of both content and portability.

MEDICAL EMERGENCIES:EVALUATION

Safety First

Always make a quick appraisal of what has happened. Do not approach an injured person unless you are absolutely sure there is no danger to yourself or others. For example, if a rockslide has occurred partially covering the casualty, more rocks may fall. If the casualty is clear of risk, approach and render assistance. If the prevailing situation continues to present further dangers to life you should carefully remove the casualty to safe ground before checking for injury.

Casualties in Danger

Much is made of spinal injuries stressing the point

of not moving casualties who have fallen. Unless you have physical evidence of a spinal injury, i.e. the casualty has fallen or received a head injury, and there is prevailing risk, the casualty should be moved to safety without undue delay. Remember to lift the casualty with great care, keeping the head in natural line with the body.

Priority of Treatment

It is often said that we can live without food for weeks, water for four days and air for four minutes. I am not so sure about the duration for food and water, but the figure for air is certainly correct. The brain needs oxygen which means the first thing you must look for is a sign of life. This means that in an emergency you should immediately check that the casualty is breathing and that a pulse is detectable. The first point indicates that the airway is clear and the second that blood is flowing around the body – at this stage nothing else is important.

In most cases, medical emergencies will be hopefully limited to individuals. However, there is always the possibility that several people have been injured at the same time. The first task in any medical emergency is to establish a process of prioritisation of the wounded. Casualties are generally sorted into categories. Those who require urgent assistance to prevent immediate death, such as those suffering from respiratory and circulatory disorders, must be given priority. Those who have suffered major body-mass loss, which results in severe haemorrhaging will also require immediate attention. While formulating your priorities, keep the following rules in mind.

EMERGENCY PRIORITIES

➤ Exclude taking any action that will put you in danger. If you become injured then you will be in no position to help anyone else.

➤ Do not panic, no matter how serious the situation may look. Take several deep breaths to calm yourself, act professionally, offer hope and encouragement.

➤ Individual casualties will need to be assessed as to their injuries. For this you will need to use all your senses – ask (if the casualty is conscious), look (and if possible feel over the body for broken bones, blood etc), listen, smell – think and act.

➤ If the casualty is conscious, they will be an important source of information. Ask them what happened and to describe their symptoms.

➤ Think about your actions first then act quickly and carefully. Boost the morale of your casualty. Offer comfort and reassurance thus building the casualty's mental strength to live.

➤ If there are any other uninjured survivors, get them to help you in any way they can. Always ask (out of earshot of any injured person) if anyone has any medical experience.

➤ Separate as soon as possible those who are saveable from those who are not.

MEDICAL EMERGENCIES: ACTIONS

To repeat the point stated above, in any emergency

situation, your primary concerns should be the casualty's ability to breath and whether their heart is beating. An easy way to remember this is the ABC routine: *Airway, Breathing, Circulation*.

Airway: Check for Breathing

If the casualty is talking, then their airway is open. To determine if an unconscious casualty is breathing, listen with your ear close to the casualty's nose and mouth. You should be able to hear and feel any breath. Watch out for chest and abdominal movement at the same time. If there is no sign of breathing, take immediate action to ensure that the casualty's air passage is clear.

If the injured person is unconscious, it may be that their airway is blocked by the position of their head, which causes the tongue to fall back in the mouth and seal the airway (pic. 1 below). To remedy this:

➤ Press down on the forehead with one hand, and with the other, lift the neck (pic. 2).

➤ Remove your hand from underneath the neck to push up the chin, to stop the tongue blocking the top of the airway (pic. 3).

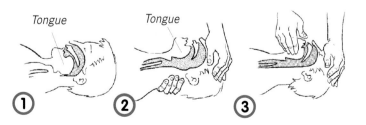

Tongue   Tongue

① ② ③

If there is still no breathing, there may be an obstruction in the airway.

➤ Turn the head to one side, keeping the chin forward and the top of the head back (pic. 1).

➤ Check quickly inside the mouth to find any other cause of blockage; place two fingers into the mouth and sweep the inside removing any blockage. e.g. dentures or vomit (pic. 2).

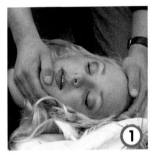

Once the air passage is open and clear, the casualty may begin breathing again. If this happens, and his heart is beating, put him into the recovery position (see p. 185). Be alert to a visible injury to the front or back of the head which might indicate damage to the neck or spine. Improvise some form of collar or head support to keep the head correctly positioned.

Breathing: Artificial Ventilation

Having checked the airway is clear, if breathing does not recommence, the casualty must be given help immediately. You must 'breathe' for them and this can best be done on a mouth-to-mouth basis (as described in the section on CPR below, see p. 180).

If the heart is beating and a pulse can be felt (see below), continue giving assisted breaths at a rate of between sixteen and eighteen a minute. When the casualty begins breathing for himself, continue giving assistance at his natural rate until breathing is normal and then place him in the recovery position (see p. 185).

If you are certain is no heartbeat, chest compression must be carried out as described below.

Circulation: Check for Heartbeat

Before starting any resuscitation it is important to check whether or not the casualty's heart is beating. Check the casualty's pulse will determine whether the heart is still beating. This can be done in either of the following ways:

➤ Using the tips of two fingers, gently slide them down the side of the casualty's Adam's apple towards the back of the neck until you feel a soft groove. Press gently on this spot. (See pic. 1)

➤ Rest your fingers lightly on the front of the wrist, about 0.5 inch (1 cm) back from the wrist joint on the thumb side , close to where a watchstrap would normally fasten.(See pic. 2)

If there is no heartbeat, chest compression must be carried out as described below. This is often done in conjunction with artificial ventilation, Together, these processes are known as CPR (cardiopulmonary resuscitation).

WARNING

➤ BE SURE that there is **NO** heartbeat before beginning chest compression. Far more harm than good will be done if attempted chest compression interferes with an existing heartbeat, however weak.

CPR

Artificial Ventilation

➤ Check breathing (look, listen, feel) and circulation response and ascertain required CPR action.

➤ Taking a deep breath, pinch the casualty's nose to prevent air loss, open your mouth wide and seal your lips around his open mouth (pic. 1).

➤ Blow into his lungs, watching for expansion of the chest (pics. 2 and 3). When the maximum expansion is reached, raise your head well clear and breathe out and in. Look now for the chest contraction (pic. 4).

➤ When this has happened, repeat the procedure once more. It may be more convenient to use mouth-to-nose contact. In this case, the casualty's mouth must be kept shut to prevent the loss of air.

➤ Following the two long assisted breaths check the carotid pulse in the neck. If breathing is absent but pulse is present, assist with rescue breathing (one breath every 5 seconds, about 12 breaths per minute). If there is no pulse, give cycles of 15 chest compressions (at a rate of around 80 to 100 compression per minute) followed by two slow breaths.

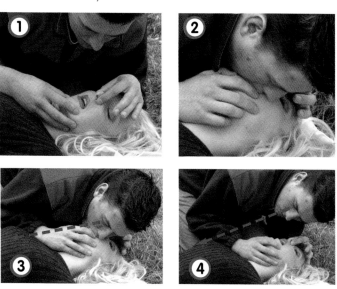

Chest Compression

➤ Check that the casualty is lying on a firm surface.

➤ Kneeling alongside, locate the bottom of the breastbone (pic. 1). Measure the width of three fingers up and place the heel of one hand on the bone. Lay the other hand over the first.

➤ Keeping the elbows rigid, lean forward so that your arms are vertical and your weight bearing down on the casualty's chest (pic. 2 overleaf).

➤ Depress the breastbone by between 4 and 5 cm

(2–2$^1/_2$ inches). Lean back to release the pressure, so allowing the breastbone to return to its original position.

➤ Perform 15 compressions at the rate of about 80 per minute. (Count, one back, two back, three back, and so on, leaning forward on each number.)

In normal conditions, breathing and circulation take place at the same time. The casualty needs both, so assisted breathing and chest compression must be carried out together. If you are alone, the procedures have to be alternated. As soon as the first 15 compressions have been given, restore the open air-passage position of the head and provide two more assisted breaths. When this has been done, continue this cycle: 15 compressions and two assisted breaths for a full minute. Then check for any heartbeat. If none is present, continue the treatment, checking for heartbeat every three minutes.

CPR By Two People

If two people are available to help, they should each provide part of the treatment with one assisting breathing, the other providing the compressions.

➤ At the start, give four assisted breaths and follow these with five compressions (pics. 1 and 2). Then establish a pattern of one assisted breath followed by five compressions. Aim at a rate of one compression per second.

➤ Each assisted breath should follow the release of the fifth compression without pause. Check for heartbeat after one minute and then after every succeeding three minutes.

➤ Discontinue compression when a pulse is felt .

➤ Continue with assisted breathing until the casualty breathes for himself.

When breathing and heartbeat are both established, place him in the recovery position (see p. 185) after checking for other injuries.

RECOVERY SIGNS

It is important to look for and recognise the recovery signs in casualties who are receiving CPR. The blueish colouring of the lips should slowly return to normal as will the facial skin tone. The pulse will return and the casualty may groan or start to move. As the casualty recovers they will resist to your CPR efforts, indicating that spontaneous breathing has returned.

> ### ABC PRIORITY CHECKLIST

➤ Casualty breathing and conscious - check for injuries.

➤ Casualty breathing and unconscious - place in recovery position (see p. 185) if injuries allow.

➤ Casualty not breathing but with chest and abdomen movement – check for airway blockage (see p. 177).

➤ Casualty not breathing with no sign of chest movement – start immediate resuscitation (see p. 179)

UNCONSCIOUSNESS

When a casualty is completely unaware of what is going on around them or is unable to make purposeful movements they are deemed to be unconscious. People who faint are briefly unconscious while those in a coma are in continuing unconsciousness. If someone collapses or you find an unconscious person, try to establish the cause. Check the immediate area to make sure it is safe before approaching the body. If someone has collapsed within a group, ask if someone noticed any prior indication of stress, such as feeling faint, chest pains. Has the casualty been drinking heavily or are they on medication? Is the casualty a know drug user? The most common causes of unconsciousness are stroke, head injury, drunkenness, poisoning and epilepsy. Check breathing and circulation and carry out CPR as necessary (see p. 179). Try talking to the casualty, if there is no response, shake them a little, although do not move them needlessly. Next assess their reaction to pain by pinching the flesh sharply. Place in the coma position (see below) until they regain consciousness or evacuation can be arranged.

THE RECOVERY POSITION

Generally, an unconscious survivor who is breathing, who has a reasonable heartbeat and who is without other injuries demanding immediate attention, should be put into the recovery (or coma) position. This position, illustrated below, is the safest because it minimizes the risk of impeded breathing. The tilted-back head ensures open air passages. The face-down attitude allows any vomit or other liquid obstruction to drain from the mouth.

The spread of the limbs will maintain the body in its position. If fractures or other injuries prevent suitable placing of the limbs, use rolled clothing or other padded objects to prop the survivor in this position.

BLEEDING

The body contains about 10 pints (5.5 litres) of blood. Damage to the body can cause blood loss, which if unchecked will weaken the circulation and blood supply to the brain. Blood will clot relatively quickly if the flow is slowed or stopped, and although a cleanly-cut blood vessel may bleed profusely if left untreated, it will also tend to shrink, close and retreat into its surrounding tissue. Sometimes these natural methods will succeed in arresting bleeding entirely unaided. It is not uncommon for mountain walkers and rock climbers to suffer minor wounds and abrasions, which should be cleaned and dressed. Any other major wound which causes severe bleeding should be stopped as soon as possible. There are three options available: direct pressure, indirect pressure and elevation.

Direct Pressure

Place a dressing over the wound and apply firm but gentle pressure with your hand. A sterile dressing is desirable (pic. 1 opposite). If one is not available, any piece of clean cloth can be used. If no dressing is ready for immediate use, cover the wound with your hand. If necessary, hold the edges of the wound together using only gentle pressure (pic. 2) or press directly on the point of bleeding (pic. 3). Any dressings should be large enough to overlap the wound and cover the surrounding area. If blood comes through the first dressing, apply a second over the first, and, if required, a third over the second. Keep an even pressure applied by tying on a firm

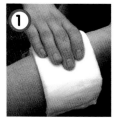

bandage. However, take care that the bandage is not so tight that, like a tourniquet, it restricts the flow of blood.

If the wound is large and suitable dressings are to hand, bring the edges of the wound together and use the dressings to keep the wound closed. To arrest the flow of blood from a very large wound, make a pad of the dressing and press it into the wound where the bleeding is heaviest. The object of this treatment is to slow down or stop the loss of blood until the body's own defences begin to work.

Elevation

If there is no danger of any other injury being aggravated, an injured limb is best raised as high as is comfortable for the casualty. This reduces the blood-flow in the limb, helps the veins to drain the area and so assists in reducing the blood-loss through the wound.

Indirect Pressure

If a combination of the above procedures does not succeed, the use of appropriate pressure points should be considered. It is necessary to recognize the type of external bleeding, because pressure points can only be used to control arterial bleeding. Arteries carry the blood outwards from the heart, in pulses of pressure. At this stage, the blood has been oxygenated and filtered of its impurities. Arterial bleeding can therefore be recognized by bright-red spurting in time with each heartbeat. In contrast, blood from the veins flows out steadily, with less pressure, and is a darker red.

A place where an artery runs across a bone near the surface of the skin constitutes a pressure point. There are four pressure points which are easily accessible to control heavy arterial bleeding, one in each limb. Those in the arms are on the brachial arteries. These run down the centre of the inner side of the upper arm (pic. 1). Pressure points for the legs are on the femoral arteries, which run down the inside of each thigh (pic. 2).

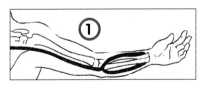
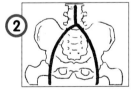

The pressure points can be found in the centre of the groin, and can be compressed against the pelvis. This is easier to do if the casualty's knee is bent. When using pressure points to control bleeding, make full use of the opportunity to dress the wound more effectively.

Pressure Application

Locate the fingers or thumb over the pressure point and apply sufficient pressure to flatten the artery and arrest the flow of blood. Redress the wound if required. Maintain the pressure for at least ten minutes to allow time for blood-clotting to begin. Do not exceed fifteen minutes. If you do, the tissues below the pressure point will begin to be damaged by the deprivation of arterial blood.

Internal Bleeding

Internal bleeding is often difficult to spot, but should be suspected if the casualty has had a hard fall on rocky ground, breaking ribs or thigh bones without external rupture of the skin. Blood appearing in the mouth, ears and nose from no obvious wound is a likely indicator, as is any excessive swelling or bruising. There is little first aid that can be applied to a casualty with internal bleeding. The best course of action is to get them to hospital as soon as possible. If you do suspect internal bleeding, treat the casualty for shock until help arrives.

SHOCK

In the context of first aid, 'shock' relates to surgical shock and has nothing to do with being frightened. Surgical shock is caused by a loss of blood circulating through the body. This causes the pressure to fall, thus inhibiting the supply of oxygen to the brain, and organs such as the heart and kidneys. The system is clever enough to monitor any blood-loss from the body and will shut down all nonessential arteries, enabling the heart and brain to operate – but there is a limit. Casualties suspected of going into shock need to be hospitalized as quickly as possible.

TREATING SHOCK

➤ Lie the casualty down and drop the head a little, allowing blood to the brain.

➤ Do not let the casualty move, and decrease all pressure on the heart.

➤ Cover the casualty very lightly. Getting the casualty too warm will only divert blood to the body's outer surface.

➤ Stop any bleeding.

➤ If the casualty is vomiting, place him in the coma or recovery position (see page ?).

➤ If breathing stops, begin artificial respiration (see p.000). Raise the legs to increase blood supply to the heart and brain.

FRACTURES

A fracture is a broken or cracked bone, which, depending on the type, may be accompanied by internal or external bleeding.

Types of Fracture

A closed fracture is not immediately obvious, although there will be swelling and bruising (pic. 1). An open fracture is where the broken bone has ruptured the skin, thus exposing the wound to infection (pic. 2). A complicated fracture may be open or closed, but where the broken bone has caused injury to nerves, arteries and other organs (pic. 3).

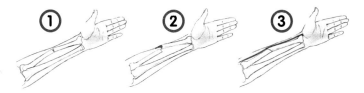

Fracture Symptoms

A bone fracture should be suspected if someone has had a serious fall and if any or all of the following signs are present:

➤ The bone is exposed through the skin.

➤ There is difficulty of normal movement in any part of the body.

➤ Increased pain when movement is attempted.

➤ Swelling or bruising accompanied by tenderness in the area of the injury.

➤ Deformity or shortening of the injured part.

➤ Grating of bone heard during examination or attempted movement.

➤ Signs of shock.

➤ The casualty has heard or felt a bone break.

Treatment

The only treatment available in an emergency situation is immobilization of the fracture. Unless some other immediate danger threatens, splint the casualty before moving him. In any case, handle him with the greatest care to avoid further pain or additional injury. If there is a wound associated with the fracture, remove the clothing in the immediate area and treat the wound before fitting splints.

Splints

Splints can be improvised from sticks and branches, or even a tight roll of clothing or bedding. Pad the splint and fasten it so that it supports the joints above and below the fracture. A fractured leg can be partially immobilized by tying it to the good leg if nothing else is available. A fractured leg may be deformed, shortened or twisted unnaturally. In such cases realignment should be attempted before immobilization, if the casualty is prepared to allow it. Carefully and gently pull the end

Arm splint

Leg splint

of the limb and reset or straighten it. When all that is possible has been done, apply the splints. The only further help that can be given is to raise the injured part to cut down swelling and discomfort, and to treat any symptoms of shock (see p. 189). If it is not possible to move the casualty, he should be allowed to rest. If it is considered that the casualty is capable of being moved, and that this provides the best way of the casualty receiving prompt hospitalization, then this should be done.

Concussion and Skull Fractures

If a survivor is even briefly unconscious, if clear or blood-tinged fluid is coming from the ears or nose, or if the pupils of the eyes are unequal or unresponsive, then a skull fracture or concussion should be suspected. If the casualty is unconscious, breathing and pulse should be monitored. If they are normal, the casualty should be placed in the recovery position (see p. 185). If the casualty is conscious, place him in a reclining position with his head and shoulders supported, keep him warm and handle him gently.

BURNS

The immediate aim when treating any burn is to lessen the ill effects of the excessive heat. Do this by gently immersing the injured part in cold water or by slowly pouring cold water over it. Persist with this treatment for ten minutes, or longer if the pain is not relieved. Cooling in this way will stop further damage, relieve pain and reduce the possibilities of swelling or shock.

Treatment

A burn opens the way for infection to enter the body, which means that a dressing should be applied. A sterile non-fluffy dressing is best, but any suitable piece of clean material will do. Dressings and bandages can be made fairly sterile by boiling, or by steaming them in a lidded container. Scorching of material will also help to kill most germs.

A solution of tannic acid will assist in the healing of burns. Tree bark boiled for as long as possible will provide this. Oak bark is the best source, but chestnut is a good alternative. Any bark will yield some tannic acid. As the water boils away, replace it with more, adding extra bark if possible. A strong-tea solution will provide the same assistance. Cool the boiled tannic acid by placing the container in cold water. Do not use any solution until it is cold.

If any restrictive clothing or other items are being worn near the burned area, remove them before any swelling develops. Do not touch the burn or use any form of adhesive dressing. If any blisters form, do not break or drain them. They are a natural protective cover for the injury and should themselves be protected. If burns or scalds are severe, lay the casualty in a comfortable position as soon as possible. If the casualty is unconscious, place him in the recovery position (see p. 189). Be aware that the patient may also go into shock (see p. 185).

Sunburn

The most likely type of burn to be encountered will be sunburn. Over-exposure to direct sunlight, especially when combined with persistent wind, can produce serious burning. Skin, wet with seawater or sweat, is similarly at risk. If sunburn does occur, protect the casualty from further exposure. Treat the area with tannic acid solution (or ointment if available), or with cold water if in plentiful supply. Then cover with a dressing. Keep the dressing in place unless it is essential that it be removed. Provide the survivor with plenty of fluids (as much as possible) and rest.

HEAT EXHAUSTION

The constant need for water arises from the fact that the body is continually releasing liquids during its normal functions, i.e. breathing, urination, excretion and sweating. It is possible for mountain walkers to suffer from heat exhaustion, which is normally caused by excessive sweating due to hot weather and arduous routes. The simple cure for this complaint is to rest in the shade, cooling the head with a water-drenched cloth while replenishing body fluids with small mouthfuls of water.

General Precautions

Wherever good water might be in short supply, the first step is to protect and conserve the water already in the body. This is done by covering any exposed skin as soon as possible. This will not only give protection against sunburn, but it will also aid water retention. Rest and avoid energetic activities until you have fully recovered. Don't smoke, or drink alcohol.

Salt Depletion

Of secondary importance to water is salt. The normal human requires 10 g each day to maintain a healthy balance. Sweat contains salt as well as water, and this salt-loss must be replaced. If it is not then you will suffer from heatstroke, heat exhaustion and muscular cramps.

Treatment

The signs of salt deficiency are sudden weakness and a hot dry sensation to the body. Place the victim in a half-lying, half-sitting position, and add a small pinch of salt to a mug of water to treat these symptoms. Fanning will also cool down the victim effectively. In hot, dry conditions it is advisable to add a small amount of salt to your entire fluid intake.

KEEPING WARM

Exposure to temperatures below freezing, especially if it is wet and windy, entails continual risk of hypothermia and frostbite. Windy conditions increase the risk of hypothermia because the cooling effects of cold air are markedly increased by its movement. Air moving at 48 km/h (30 mph) and having a temperature of -20°C (-4°F) has the same chilling effect as air at -40°C (-40°F) moving at only 8 km/h (5 mph). Wet conditions increase the danger because wet cold air is a better conductor of heat, and can therefore carry more away from the body. In addition, many of the insulating properties of clothing are lost if garments are wet or damp.

The Layer System

Make the most efficient use of all available clothing. Remember that a number of thinner layers are more effective than one or two thick heavy garments in preventing loss of body heat. The aim is to maintain a layer of unchanging air close to your body. Tight clothing should therefore be avoided. Adjust your clothing so as to reduce sweating. Too much perspiration lowers the insulating efficiency of clothing, as well as cooling the skin as the sweat evaporates. Remove layers of clothing and/or open garments at the front, wrist or neck to get the right balance. Do everything possible to prevent clothing getting wet, and do all you can to dry it if it does get wet.

Hands and Feet

Take special care of hands and feet. They are the limits of circulation and can lose heat very rapidly. Do everything possible to ensure that the fastenings at wrists, ankles, neck and around the waist are efficient without restricting the circulation of blood. Keep hands under cover whenever possible, warming them under the armpits or between the thighs when necessary. If toes are nipped by frost, warm them against a companion if possible. If alone, warm toes by wriggling them, moving the feet and, providing there are no serious signs, gentle massage.

Make every effort to keep feet dry. If spare socks are available, keep some close to hand so that a change into a dry pair can be made at least once a day. Periodically remove footwear and rub your feet for up to ten minutes. Try to improvise over-boots using plastic bags placed over walking boots to ensure extra insulation against cold and wet.

HYPOTHERMIA

This general condition of the body is caused when it loses heat more quickly than heat can be replaced. Among the conditions likely to produce an increased risk of hypothermia are cold, wet weather, wet clothing, immersion in cold water, exhaustion, inadequate clothing and a shortage of food or drink. Hypothermia is not an easily-diagnosed condition. It is important, therefore, to keep a special lookout if you are subject to any of these conditions.

HYPOTHERMIA SYMPTOMS

➤ Paleness and severe uncontrollable shivering.
➤ Being subnormally cold to the touch.
➤ Muscular weakness and fatigue.
➤ Drowsiness and dimming of sight.
➤ Diminishing heartbeat and breathing.
➤ Eventual collapse and unconsciousness (extremely serious).

Perhaps the most striking indication of the onset of hypothermia is that of a marked change in the personality of the sufferer. An extrovert may become an introvert. Aggressiveness may change to

Body heat transfer is one of the most effective treatments for hypothermia.

submission, or vice versa. What is certain is that hypothermia is deadly unless it is treated. The treatment of hypothermia is centred on stopping the loss of body heat and replacing lost warmth.

HYPOTHERMIA TREATMENT

➤ Do not rub or massage to stimulate circulation.

➤ Do not warm the casualty by using external fire or heat.

➤ Do not permit the casualty further exertion.

➤ Provide shelter from the wind and cold as soon as possible.

➤ If dry clothing or covering is available, use it to replace any wet clothing.

➤ Replace wet clothing in stages, uncovering as little of the body as possible at any one time.

➤ If no dry clothing is available, leave any wet garments on and get the casualty into a sleeping bag or survival bag (a, see p.000). It should be wind- and waterproof, as well as being reflective of radiated body heat.

➤ Provide body warmth. Another healthy survivor is a good source and can share the survival bag. If the casualty is conscious, provide hot food and drink. If none is available, eat chocolate or high-energy food. Do not give alcohol.

There are two other actions to remember if hypothermia is encountered. If both breathing and heartbeat are undetectable, artificial ventiation (see p. 180) and chest compressions (see p. 181) will need to be administered. Do not assume death from hypothermia, unless your efforts have achieved normal body temperature and the casualty still does not revive. Handle any hypothermia survivor gently. Frozen skin and flesh are very easily damaged.

CRAMP

The onset of cramp is very sudden and starts with an involuntary contraction of the lower leg muscles, normally those in the calf. They can occur at any time, but are most prevalent after very strenuous exercise, when you are resting. Cramps are more frequent after walking in hot weather, when heavy sweating has occurred. Although extremely painful, the condition is not serious and the pain will dissipate within a few minutes.

Treatment

Any joint that is bent by the cramping muscles should be gently straightened. Massaging the affected area with a gentle stroking movement should then help to relieve the tension.

BLISTERS

Normally, blisters are considered a minor injury and are treated as such. However, when out walking the pain of a blister can become disabling and out of all proportion to its medical significance. Blisters on the feet are usually caused by ill-fitting boots, poor-quality socks or loose laces combined with long periods of having to walk over rough, uneven ground.

Bad blisters can be avoided. First of all, the feet must

be kept clean and dry, washed whenever possible, dried thoroughly and foot powder applied. If you notice sore spots on your feet while walking, put some surgical spirit on them to toughen them up.

Treatment

As soon as you feel a blister beginning, stop immediately and treat the problem. Put some antiseptic cream on the sore area and then cover it with surgical dressing, without making any creases in the tape. If the sore area is on a toe, use micropore tape instead. If a blister has already formed, use a blister ring so that pressure is kept off the affected area.

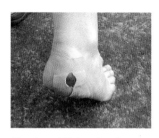

Create a blister ring to relieve the pressure on the affected area

Severe Blisters

A severe blister is often filled with fluid, and can be made more comfortable if the fluid is removed. To do this, do not burst it, as this leaves a larger area open to infection, but pierce it at the bottom edge using a sterilized needle. If possible, wash the foot thoroughly first, then gently express the fluid and cover the blister with a blister ring. Make sure that the dressing is changed daily and the area cleaned. A footbath of hot, salty water is healing, comforting and helps to harden the skin. However, make sure that the area is thoroughly dried. Blisters heal best when they are kept clean and dry.

CARBON MONOXIDE (CO) POISONING

Carbon monoxide poisoning is produced when incomplete combustion of fuel takes place. In an unventilated enclosure, such as a tent, it can quickly become lethal. The breathing of such fumes in a confined space instigates death by asphyxia within 15 to 20 minutes. The gas is odourless, colourless and tasteless, making it difficult to detect.

The warning signs include a build-up of pressure in the head, followed by confusion, vomiting, convulsions and coma. All those suspected of suffering from carbon monoxide poisoning should be removed from possible exposure (e.g. a stove in a tent) and examined.

The same degree of poisoning may affect individuals sharing accommodation with differing degrees of the same symptoms. This variation in individuals is a classic sign of carbon monoxide poisoning.

CO POISONING SYMPTOMS

➤ headache
➤ bounding pulse
➤ dilated pupils
➤ As the level of poisoning increases the skin especially the lips may deepen to cherry pink.
➤ The casualty maybe confused and breathing impaired. In the advanced stages unconsciousness may develop.

Treatment

The best remedy against carbon monoxide poisoning is prevention.

➤ Always ensure good ventilation if using an oil burning stove.
➤ Check any manufactured stove, and maintain its clean running.
➤ Always turn off or extinguish any petrol or aviation type stove before going to sleep.

For those suspected of carbon monoxide poisoning, the treatment is to maximise oxygenation. In the wilderness this means removing the casualty from any source of contamination and placing them in the fresh air. If unconscious but breathing, place them in the recovery position (see p. 185). Where breathing has stopped, start CPR (see p. 180). Give 100 per cent oxygen if available. Evacuate to a medical facility where high oxygen absorption can be provided more efficiently. If evacuation is delayed, monitor breathing, pulse, and responsiveness at ten-minute intervals.

DROWNING AND NEAR DROWNING

Wilderness activities present many problems; one primary example is river crossing (see p. 75) and the risk of drowning. Drowning is defined as death resulting from suffocation. This is caused by total (mouth and nose) submersion in water for a duration long enough to stop the heart. If the duration is not of sufficient time to totally extinguish all life signs and the casualty can be revived, this is termed as near drowning.

Treatment

Swim or wade out to the victim as quickly as possible. Remove any obstructions from the airway and begin mouth-to-mouth resuscitation (see p. 180). This should start and continue while still in the water. When ashore place the casualty on a firm surface and check breathing and heartbeat – continue with CPR for as long as required. Do not worry about getting the casualty to heave up any swallowed water.

Once spontaneous breathing has returned place the casualty in the recovery position and cover with a blanket. If the water is very cold, check for hypothermia (see p. 198). Continue to monitor the casualty very ten minutes until they are evacuated.

LIGHTNING INJURY

High mountains have a nasty habit of attracting lightning. It is wise to take precautions against lightning although it is very rare for an electrical storm to occur without some advance warning such as the appearance of thunderclouds in the distance followed by flashes of lightning and rumbles of thunder as the clouds approach. Be aware that lightning striking the ground normally seeks the easiest point to make contact which is usually the highest point in the area.

Such is the power of lightning that a direct strike will

almost certainly produce death by cardiac arrest because it disrupts all normal cardiac activity. Those surviving will suffer from any or all of the following symptoms:

LIGHTNING STRIKE SYMPTOMS

➤ Temporary paralysis is common.
➤ Burns due to wet skin or metal jewellery.
➤ Injury to the eyes and ears.
➤ Fractured bones.
➤ Memory loss.

In a lightning storm if caught out in the open it is much safer to stay in the open, even if it is in driving rain. Sit down, preferably on your rucksack, and minimise your contact points with the ground as much as possible by drawing your knees up and placing your hands in your lap.

Lightning is almost always accompanied by rain and wherever possible you should avoid both by finding shelter in a strong structure such as a cave or rock overhang. Staying dry will prevent skin burn if you are unfortunate enough to be struck. Stay away from mountain peaks where the danger of lightning strikes is greatly increased. Injury to anyone struck by lightning will depend on how long they were exposed and how wet they were at the time. Those struck by lightning must be treated quickly.

Treatment

Casualties who have been hit by a lightning strike fall into three categories: totally crisped (dead), unconscious and conscious. Those that are unconscious should be attended to first. Lightning often causes the heart and respiration to stop and it is therefore vital to check for breathing and heartbeat. Those that are breathing should not be moved because lightning can easily fracture the neck and backbone. If the casualty is not breathing, start CPR immediately (see p. 180). Unlike other instances (such as heart attack) your CPR efforts should continue as long as it is physically possible. Those that are conscious, screaming and running about like a banshee are going to be all right. They may be suffering from any of the above symptoms, all of which can be dealt with in order of priority.

Treat any burns as described on p. 193. Most of the burns will be on exposed or wet skin. However, in certain cases the lightning may cause a burn strip down the entire length of the body, which is not normally very deep. Check for individual puncture-type burns, which are normally a lot deeper but small enough in size to be treated without immediate hospitalisation. Confusion and short-term memory loss are fairly common, and although conscious the casualty may also suffer from temporary paralysis.

HIGH ALTITUDE SICKNESS (HAS)

An illness occurring for those who walk, ski or climb in high mountains (also known as acute mountain sickness) as a result of reduced oxygen in the air. Although the proportion of oxygen (21 per cent) in the atmosphere remains the same at all altitudes, the air becomes much thinner the higher you go, resulting in less available oxygen. At 1,500 m (5,000 ft) the oxygen is 80 per cent of its value at sea level. While this might not seem significant, it starts to starve the muscles of oxygen and makes physical activity difficult. Humans have difficulty operating in oxygen levels of less than 70 per cent of norm, because the breathing rate has to be increased to compensate, which in turn reduces the amount of carbon dioxide removed from the blood.

The symptoms can appear within a few hours when at a height of around 2,100 m (7,000 ft). The higher and quicker you go, the greater the symptoms. The age of the affected individual also makes a difference to the speed with which these symptoms begin to be felt.

HAS SYMPTOMS

➤ Nausea

➤ Headache

➤ Vomiting and rapid heartbeat

➤ Breathing becomes increasingly difficult

The sickness becomes dangerous if allowed to persist, leading to an increased intensity of the symptoms and the additional loss of balance and difficulty in walking. Above 2,400 m (8,000 ft) the lungs can become filled with a frothy fluid – pulmonary edema – resulting in compromised air exchange and shortness of breath.

Treatment

Altitude sickness can be prevented by acclimatization prior to your excursion, but this can take several weeks. Where acclimatisation has not taken place slowing the rate of ascent will help the body adjust. Oxygen may be given as an emergency treatment but the only real cure is a slow descent to a safe altitude.

FOREST FIRES

A major threat to all those who venture into remote mountainous areas is that of forest fires. Forest fires have been known to start as a result of a rock fall, lightning and natural combustion. However, the most common cause comes from careless humans: discarded cigarettes, camp fires and the misuse of pyrotechnics are but a few ways in which fire can start. A forest fire will spread and burn depending on two main factors: material to consume (fuel) and wind (oxygen). In a forest fire the material is either ground cover or trees, a combination which

can produce enough heat to cause flashover.
Flashover occurs when the material in the path of the
fire is preheated so that it is instantly combustible,
making the fire continuous. For this reason fire lanes
are cut to starve the fire of fuel. The wind will dictate
the direction of the fire and its speed. A full-blown
forest fire is an amazing spectacle but is it also very
dangerous.

Caught in a Forest Fire

If a forest fire is detected you must move out of its
path. Check the prevailing wind direction to
determine which way the fire is travelling. If you are
on high ground you will be able to see the movement.
The main risk is when the fire is advancing towards
you; walk at a 90° angle to the fire and aim where
possible for the flattest ground. Hills and gullies can
take time to climb and are also areas where the fires
move the swiftest. Remember that in addition to the
fire, smoke inhalation is also a killer.

CARRYING AN INJURED PERSON

A moderately injured person should be carried
between two helpers, using whichever handgrip suits
best or by a fireman's lift. The lifts illustrated overleaf
are the four-handed seat (pic. 1), used when the
injured person can use his arms, and the two-handed
seat (pic. 2), for when the injured person is unable to
use his arms. Another option is to empty a rucksack
and extend the shoulder straps to the limit. It is then
possible to piggy-back the casualty by threading his
legs through the straps of the rucksack by getting him

to hold onto you around your neck. This is only viable, though, if the casualty is able to hold on. However, a more seriously injured person, if they must be moved, should be moved in such a way as not to endanger their health or worsen their injuries further. In these cases, a stretcher, even an improvised one, should be used. A makeshift stretcher can be made by threading two fastened jackets poles or branches, with a belt to give more stability at the middle. If you have to lift a casualty to get them on a stretcher, make sure that the body is kept straight and that each part is well supported. If there are any suspected spinal injuries, do not attempt to move them.

PRECAUTIONS AGAINST THINGS THAT BITE

No adventurer into the wilderness should make the

mistake of thinking that the greatest danger comes from large animals. Some countries, such as Great Britain, have very little wild game, few snakes or other reptiles. If anything, it is the smaller forms of wildlife that should give most cause for concern. Any insect bite is potentially dangerous.

Mosquitoes

 Mosquitoes, while not particularly dangerous in the Arctic and temperate regions, can be deadly in the Tropics. They can carry malaria, yellow fever and filariasis. Do everything possible to gain protection against their bites. Use mosquito netting or repellent constantly if it is available. If not, cover any exposed skin with handkerchiefs or anything else to hand. Even large leaves will help. Wear full clothing, especially at night. Keep trouser legs tucked into the tops of socks and shirt sleeves into gloves or other improvised hand covering. Smear the face and other exposed skin with mud before bedding down for the night. Select rest sites or camps which are clear of and higher than swampy ground or stagnant or sluggish water, since this is where mosquitoes breed. . There is no immunization against malaria, so any anti-malaria drugs must be used as directed for as long as they last.

Biting Gnats and Midges

Apart from the irritation caused by clouds of midges

hovering around your head, there are several species of blood-sucking gnats that feed on livestock. These are of particular importance as they can transmit disease from animals to humans, though this is rare in the Western world.

Avoiding Midges

Stay away from areas which have recently housed livestock, especially during the hours of dusk. Likewise, avoid any standing water because this is a common breeding ground for gnats and midges. A liberal layer of insect repellent will normally stop any actual bites, but in areas of high infestation you might consider covering any exposed skin, such as the face, with a fine mesh hood.

Ticks

Ticks are crawling creatures measuring between 2 mm and 1 cm. They are bloodsuckers and possess strong piercing jaws, and are responsible for most of the world's transmittable diseases. There are two families of ticks which are able to transmit disease to humans. *Soft ticks* hide in dilapidated buildings where there is poor hygiene. They usually are active at night and bite sleeping people. *Hard ticks* normally feed on animals, e.g. dogs, goats, rats, sheep, cattle, onto which they climb from the ground or vegetation. They can transmit tick typhus from animals to humans.

Avoiding Ticks

Preventing ticks from attaching themselves to you is the best way of avoiding tick-transmitted disease.

Unless it is an emergency, you should not sleep in old buildings which have housed livestock. If you are camping out, ensure that the vegetation around the tent is kept short. Hard ticks are the most common but any disease will not be transferred if the tick is removed within 24 hours. Most DEET insect repellents are very effective against ticks.

Removing a Tick

The best method of removal is to grasp the skin area around the tick's body with a pair of fine-point tweezers, and remove the tick with a sharp backwards pull. This does not hurt and is a far safer method than trying to induce the tick to disengage itself by any other method. Burning the tick or applying chemicals will only force the tick to vomit, and crushing it will cause germs to enter the victim.

Flies, Bees, Wasps and Hornets

There are many species of fly which can transmit a wide range of diseases. However, good camp and personal hygiene will prevent most contamination.

All bees, wasps and hornets are very dangerous if aroused. Nests are generally brownish oval or oblong masses, on tree trunks or branches between 3 m (9 ft) and 10 m (30 ft) above ground. Avoid them if possible. If a swarm is disturbed, and you are nearby, sit still for five minutes or so, and then crawl away slowly and carefully. Should you be attacked, run through the bushiest undergrowth you can find. This will beat off the insects as it springs back. Immersion in water is another defence.

Snakes

In the UK there is only one species of poisonous snake – the adder. In America the coral snake, copperhead, rattlesnake and cottonmouth are the snakes which should concern the walker. A

snakebite is seldom life-threatening, but you should take a number of precautions just to be on the safe side. As snakes strike at ankle level you should wear boots and socks which protect the lower part of your leg. In America in particular, ensure that you do not walk at night, as snakes are nocturnal. They also like to seek out warm places at night, so a tent is far preferable to sleeping out under the stars. In the unlikely event of being bitten by a snake, the best thing to do is to tie a bandage above the bite, then gradually cover the bite with the bandage and tie it again firmly below the bite. Get medical assistance as soon as possible, and certainly within twelve hours.

Bears

America is home to black bears and grizzly bears. In both cases it is best to avoid them if at all possible. You can do this by making a noise such as singing or talking as you are walking along, and by avoiding anything which looks like rotting food, as this may well be a bear larder.

If you encounter a bear, do not look it in the eye. If it turns sideways on to you or starts to shake its head from side to side, it is inviting you to leave. Move away very slowly and very quietly. Never run, as a grizzly bear can run far faster than you. Often, a bear charge will in fact be a bluff. Standing absolutely still may well help your cause. As a last resort, play dead by rolling yourself into a ball, drawing your legs up into your torso and covering your neck with your hands.

POISONOUS PLANTS

In the USA, poison sumac (pic. 1), poison oak (pic. 2) and poison ivy (pic. 3) all cause skin irritation. If your skin comes into contact with any of these plants, you should wash the affected area with soap and water, and remove and wash any affected clothing. Remember not to touch any other parts of your skin or face until you have

thoroughly washed. If you are very allergic, and the rash persists for a number of weeks, see a doctor who will prescribe medication which should help combat the symptoms.

The Weather

The weather at best is unpredictable and this is doubly so in high mountainous regions. Weather can cause many problems and potential dangers for both mountain walkers and rock climbers, so you must be aware of sudden changes at all times and be prepared to act accordingly. Although we cannot change the weather, we can to a certain extent anticipate it.

Before undertaking any trek into a wilderness area check out the weather forecast for the region. Any weather conditions that are liable to cause exposure and frostbite or heatstroke are good reasons for postponing your activity. Always use common sense and try to interpret prevailing weather conditions in the light of the most up-to-date forecast. This becomes even more important in winter. Fatalities which occur as a result of the weather often involve some human careless-ness or ignorance.

WEATHER PROBLEMS

You should be aware that the weather can pose a whole range of problems many of which can be life-threatening.

Rain

Heavy rain can cause streams to become fast and swollen. Trying to negotiate a swollen stream is very risky, so find another route if necessary to detour around it (see p. 75).

Fog

Fog can be dangerous as it is disorientating and hides obstacles and hazards, such as cliff edges. In such terrain and conditions you are best advised to stay put until the visibility improves. If you have to keep going, consider roping the members of the party together. In this way you can be assured that no one will get lost and it may also save someone from a nasty fall.

Wind

Wind gusts, especially in exposed places such as a high ridge-line, can be so powerful as to knock a person off their feet. If there is any danger of this, get all party members to crawl on their hands and knees and keep them close together. Again, it may be necessary to rope everyone together.

Hailstones

Hailstones can be up to 2 cm (1 in) in diameter and can rain down with sufficient force to cause injury. In the rare event of being caught out in a hailstorm, make sure you find shelter or at least cover your head.

Lightning

It is wise to take precautions against lightning whenever you venture into the mountains. However, it is very rare for an electrical storm to occur without some advance warning. The appearance of thunderclouds in the distance followed by flashes of lightning and rumbles of thunder are all good indicators. Watch the direction in which the clouds are moving. Note that lightning strikes the easiest point with which to make contact, which is usually the highest point in the area. If you are caught out in a lightning storm, it is much safer to stay out in the open, even if it is in driving rain. Sit down, preferably on your rucksack, and minimize your contact points with the ground by drawing your knees up and placing your hands in your lap.

WEATHER FORECASTS

In addition to the national television, radio and newspaper weather forecasts, everyone has access to a number of other forecasting services. While it is impossible to mention all those in America and Europe, those in Great Britain are mentioned here as examples.

Weathercall offers forecasts by telephone or by fax.

For instance, to get a regional telephone forecast for northwest Scotland, you should ring 0891 500 425, for north Wales 0891 500 415 and for the Lake District 0891 500 419. Similarly, fax forecasts are available for these areas by typing 0897 300 1, plus the appropriate suffix (northwest Scotland is 25), into the fax machine. Weathercall also provides a national seven-day forecast by phone on 0891 500 400. Regional long-range forecasts are also available.

There are also specialized weather forecasts for mountain walkers. BBC Radio Scotland has a daily forecast at 6.55 pm (weekdays) and 6.05 pm (weekends), and in winter this includes an avalanche risk assessment as well. ClimbLine provides regional forecasts for the Western Highlands of Scotland on

AUTHOR'S NOTE

➤   I have found a method of anticipating any immediate danger from the weather. A clear sky with high cloud will indicate a clear and sunny day. Dark sky with low cloud normally indicates rain. It is simply a matter of gauging the degree between the two. I do this by looking towards my direction of travel and try to estimate the height of cloud, colour of sky and wind direction. With a little practice one is able to anticipate the weather conditions for several hours ahead.

0891 333 198 and the Eastern Highlands on 0891 333 197. Most youth hostels in mountainous areas get a faxed daily forecast from the Met Office.

Search and Rescue

Providing the right protection is in place mountain walking and traditional rock climbing are not dangerous pastimes, but the wilderness can be quite isolated, and while in the normal course of events this adds to the attraction, it also adds to the risk. Unfortunately, if you are injured or become immobilized, or get caught in unexpected rough weather, this isolation can hamper attempts to locate and rescue you. Luckily, both America and Europe support excellent search and rescue organizations. You can also drastically reduce the time they take to find you by sticking to some basic procedures.

AUTHOR'S NOTE

➤ You should always check on what rescue services are available and whether they are free or if a fee is payable. Although the rescue services in Great Britain are free, in some European countries you can be charged by the minute for any rescue, and that is very expensive. I would advise you to take out insurance in such countries.

INJURY

If an accident does happen, the most important thing is to keep a cool head and not be panicked into a decision which could make the situation even worse. If you are in a party, the leader should keep calm and keep the rest of the party calm and under control too. First, assess the situation and check for any danger to yourself or others before approaching any casualty. If the casualty has fallen, be very careful about approaching from above as this may cause rocks to be dislodged on top of him.

Once the casualty has been reached, make a quick but thorough check for any injuries or conditions that may be life-threatening (see p. 176). Assess if there are further dangers in the immediate area, either to the casualty, yourself or other members of the party. If so, are you able to move the patient without further injury? At all costs avoid unnecessary treatments or moving the patient when there is any danger of spinal injury. It is important to keep the patient as comfortable and as warm as possible, so if shelter and a source of warmth are available, make use of them, ensuring that the casualty is well insulated.

Quickly assess if the situation is life-threatening or not. High blood-loss or acute respiratory failure will require prompt removal of the casualty to hospital if he is to survive. If the injury is serious, such as a spinal injury, specialized medical assistance will be required before the casualty can be moved. In these cases, outside help in the form of a mountain rescue team will be needed.

LOST

In the short term, simply getting lost does not pose a major problem. If you realize that you have made a map-reading error and aren't where you wanted to be, then you aren't technically lost – just misplaced! Try to work out your position on the map and adjust your route accordingly. If it is not possible to do this but you can see where you want to go, you should proceed. This may well involve retracing your steps or going downhill, but not necessarily. If this is not possible, due to fog, mist or lack of daylight, consider finding a camp site and erecting your tent, or finding an emergency shelter (see p. 90). It is up to the individual or party leader to make a decision as to whether to move on or stay put, based on the weather conditions and the terrain.

Being lost for any length of time is normally due to prevailing weather conditions, which not only hamper you and your party, but also any rescue operation. Providing you are not injured, and there are no casualties in your group, the main concern will be protection against hypothermia (see p.198).

FEAR

Fear is an entirely normal, and sometimes necessary,

emotion. It is the instinctive reaction of anyone faced with the uncertain or unknown, especially if there is a threat to life. Behaviour and reaction are always influenced by fear, and, through them, so are the prospects for survival. Fear can make people do silly things and you could end up with more casualties. It is no good trying to hide from the situation; if you try to cover up in a party of people, it will create an atmosphere of distrust. It is always best to let everyone know the real situation in a calm, optimistic and confident manner. Keep them involved and busy at all levels, from planning the course of action to helping any casualties. Idleness will only allow for reflection on any fears or discomfort.

Acceptance of fear as a natural reaction to any threatening situation will produce two immediate and positive benefits:

➤ You will be able to dismiss the fear of being afraid, which is often a burden in itself. True courage may be found in people who freely admit to fear, and then go on to do their best in the circumstances they face.

➤ You will find yourself more likely to be able to carry out considered rather than uncoordinated actions. You will recognize that there is always something that can be done to improve the situation – never give up hope.

SHELTER AND SURVIVAL

When forced to stay put either through injury, being

lost or being caught out in extreme weather conditions, you should erect your tent or seek some form
of shelter if you are to avoid exposure. Tents are by
far the quickest and best form of protection, but
survival shelters need not be complicated, or take too
much time or energy to construct (see p. 90). In the
most basic terms, you could construct a windbreak
from roots or branches, shelter beneath trees and dig
a snow trench if appropriate, or wrap yourself in a
sleeping bag or spare blanket. You should, if possible,
choose your camp site or create your shelter well
before dark. Always check the location thoroughly to
make sure that it isn't in a place liable to flooding,
that there is no danger of a rock fall and that there
are no overhanging trees that might fall in a high
wind. Keep your shelter small, as this will make it cosy.
If you plan to light a fire inside, ensure that you have
sufficient ventilation to avoid carbon monoxide
poisoning (p. 202). Always insulate the ground below
your body because sleeping on the earth will quickly
rob you of heat.

SURVIVAL KIT

If you are forced to
construct some form of
shelter your personal
survival pack will be of the
utmost importance. It
should be carried at all
times when the potential
for a survival situation
exists. Survival kits can be

DIY SURVIVAL KIT

➤ **Matches.** A dozen or more kitchen matches, which have been completely immersed in melted candle wax to make them waterproof and wind-resistant. They should be carried in a waterproof container.

➤ **Candle.** A 10 cm (4 in) candle weighs less than 25 g (1 oz) yet will burn for up to three hours if it is protected from the wind (see p. 108).

➤ **Compass.** A compass is a priority item for your kit. A button compass is the ideal choice. It is easy to read but takes up the minimum amount of space.

➤ **Needle.** A needle with a large eye, about 5 cm (2 in) long (e.g. Chenille no. 16 or a sail-maker's needle), can be used for heavy-duty sewing of materials such as shoe leather, rawhide or heavy clothing. It can also be magnetized for use as a pointer in an improvised compass.

➤ **Survival bag.** One of the most frequent dangers to be faced in a survival situation is the involuntary loss of critical amounts of body-heat. This loss occurs through convection, conduction or radiation. A survival bag is therefore a must (see p. 97).

➤ **Water purification tablets.** These provide a quick and convenient way of sterilizing water. Each tablet will purify 1 litre (2 pints) of water in about ten minutes.

➤ **Knife.** A Swiss Army-type knife, incorporating a wide variety of functions, is best. It can include extra blades, scissors, can and bottle openers, screwdriver and saw among its many implements. It is strongly recommended that a small pocket knife is carried as a matter of course.

➤ **Parachute cord.** Many a farmer will tell you that he never goes out without a quantity of string in his pocket. The same principle should apply to everyone who travels in the wilderness, except you would be better off using a 15 m (45 ft) length of parachute cord.

➤ **Flares.** In a survival situation, signal flares attract attention better than most other methods.

purchased ready-made and are designed to suit various activities and environments. You may well feel you need to build your own survival kit based on your own experiences and needs. Your decision on the items to be included should be made purely on each item's usefulness, and its adaptability in relation to your type of mountain walking activities. This assessment should be made keeping in mind the strong possibility that the survival kit may be your only initial resource. However, any survival item acts as a catalyst for prompting action and calming fear. Listed below are a selection of possible components for a personal survival kit, together with notes on their uses. The items mentioned are those which I strongly recommend for inclusion. You may find others which are useful in a particular situation.

GOING FOR HELP

If you have a problem and need help, visually check the area for other walking or climbing groups nearby. If none is contactable and the party is equipped with a mobile phone, this should be used (if reception is clear) to get in touch with the rescue services.

However, you may well have to send members of the party for help. If you do decide to send others, send at least two. These people must be fit, reliable and know exactly what is expected of them. There should be enough daylight hours in order for them to reach the nearest rescue post. You should also instruct them on the best route of how to get there or the nearest place from which the rescue services can be contacted. The messengers should be aware that the rescue depends on their getting through safely and that speed is not as important as their safety. Do not expect them to commit all the relevant knowledge to memory but instead write it on a note to carry with them. The note should contain the following information.

RESCUE NOTE

➤ Your location, with a six-figure grid reference (see p. 64).

➤ The type of terrain you are in, with details of the best approach route.

➤ Relevant details of any injured party.

➤ A summary of your plan of action so far.

➤ The type of help required. If their point of first contact is a telephone, they must use this to contact the rescue services, police, etc.

ALONE

If you are alone, conscious and your injuries do not

prevent you from walking, then you should evaluate your situation carefully before moving. This evaluation will be the same as that for a group. If no one near you can be contacted, you should balance the dangers and the value of attempting to seek help with those of staying put and letting the rescue services find you.

Make sure any casualty left alone on the hills is equipped to signal rescuers

If you are immobile and unable to walk, the decision will be made for you. In this event you should do all within your capabilities to protect yourself from the elements and prepare some form of signal device with which to attract attention. If you have a tent but are unable to erect it, try folding it around your body. If, due to your injuries, you can only achieve the prone position, do all that is possible to insulate yourself from the ground. In bad visibility, the odds are that any rescue party will be on foot, so blow a whistle at frequent intervals.

Sometimes it is necessary to leave casualties on their own while help is summoned, but this must be considered only as a last resort. An unconscious casualty should never be left alone as his condition may deteriorate very quickly, and without the rendering of immediate first aid he may die. In any case where a casualty is left alone, all possible measures must be taken to ensure his comfort, health and safety. The casualty should be given strict instructions not to move, as this will hamper any rescue attempt. Make sure some form of signal device is left with the casualty, and that you mark the area with something brightly coloured fixed firmly to the ground.

If it happens that the group leader is injured, and left alone, he must ensure before sending others to fetch help that they speak to the relevant people, preferably the leader of the rescue team, or contact the emergency services. They then must ensure that all relevant information is clearly and accurately given when requested, and that any requests from the rescue team are obeyed.

MOUNTAIN RESCUE TEAMS

Mountain rescue teams are available throughout America and Europe, but I will use those of Great Britain as an example. There are about a hundred in the British Isles and they are well organized and well equipped. They work in collaboration with the Royal Air Force and the police in search and rescue operations and training. Local mountain rescue teams also run and maintain mountain rescue posts, identified by an MR sign. It is from these bases that a rescue is normally mounted, although this is not always the case. Some posts, due to their remote nature, are unmanned, but still carry most of the equipment and supplies to enable a rescue attempt to be made.

Search Patterns

When searching for a missing individual or party, the rescue services will react to whatever information is available. If the location of an accident is known, a small advance party will be sent out first. These reconnaissance units will consist of three or four very experienced members, who will have an excellent working knowledge of the area. In addition, helicopters and search dogs, should they be required, can be called upon. Advance parties are often lightly equipped, carrying just basic first aid, shelter kits, food and radios. They follow the last-known route of the lost party or will search in any likely places of refuge. Once the casualty has been found, they will provide immediate care, and organize a stretcher party if a helicopter is not available.

If the location is not known, the search and rescue (SAR) services will separate into small mobile teams. The area covered will be based on the best estimated overall guide of the missing person's last-known location. How the search is carried out will be determined by the size of the area to be covered, the terrain, the weather and operational necessity. If you have followed the correct procedures and notified others of your intended route, or you can establish radio or telephone communication, a contact search will be initiated. This is designed to concentrate rescue efforts on a relatively small area, thus increasing the speed at which rescuers can get to you.

Unless there is accurate knowledge of the location of the party to be rescued, it would be futile and even risky to send a search team out at night. However, certain refuge points, such as mountain huts and bothies, will sometimes be checked. At times, when there is no known route or precise location, the mountain rescue teams may establish a forward base where stretchers and heavier equipment can be left, while searches continue using one of four main methods:

SEARCH TYPES

➤ **Area search** This involves dividing up the area into smaller sections using natural features as landmarks. These provide boundaries within which individual teams can search.

➤ **Sweep search** The rescue party spreads out in a line and searches the area in a disciplined and organized manner.

➤ **Contact search** A search focused on a smaller area but based on the principles of the sweep search.

➤ **Dog search** The advantage of search dogs is that they work using their sense of smell rather than sight, and are capable of tracking ground scent for up to 48 hours, and even longer in ideal conditions. If required, search dogs can work as well in the dark as they can in the light.

HELICOPTER MOUNTAIN RESCUE OPERATIONS

As mentioned earlier, mountain rescue teams in Britain are highly skilled and have access to excellent resources, including RAF helicopters and front-line medical care. However, it would be a dangerous mistake to assume that they will always be there to get you out of danger. For various reasons, such as the rescue team not knowing your location or serious weather conditions, the team may not always be able to get to you in time. Therefore, it is always better to have a

good degree of self-reliance, so that your chances of survival in an emergency will be increased. If you set out with an attitude of independence and competence, then not only will you be able to help yourself in an emergency, but you will also be able to aid others in distress.

With forethought and the correct equipment and skills, the experienced individual or leader of a party should be able to deal with most emergency situations that arise. However, even with the best planning and the most experienced people, accidents can still happen, and even a minor injury or incident, when it happens in the mountains, can often become something far worse if the correct procedures are not followed.

The team leader should be aware that a helicopter

will take some time to carry out a rescue, as strict safety procedures must be adhered too. Helicopter crews can take a considerable amount of time assessing the possible problems that may be encountered in a mountainous rescue site. It is not uncommon on very windy days for a pilot to have several attempts at establishing a hover close enough to the casualty to be able to get a winch man or mountain rescue team to their position. Having arrived at a workable hover, the next priority is to assess the safest method of rescuing the casualty. To ensure no important aspect of the situation is overlooked, RAF crews use a standardized system of assessment and briefing.

The following priorities normally govern the decision-making process:

➤ Aircraft safety
➤ Winch man safety
➤ Survivor safety

It may seem odd to place the casualty at the bottom of the priority list, but there is little justification for endangering the lives of several rescuers unless the situation demands it. Rescue attempts are, therefore, all about risk assessment.

SIGNALLING

One of the first priorities in any survival situation is

communication. If at all possible, the survivor must let the outside world know that he needs help. Check whatever means of communication is available to you. If you have a mobile phone which is receiving a signal, it could place you in direct communication with a helicopter winchman. (I am reliably informed that most RAF winchmen carry a mobile phone during any rescue operation. If you are carrying a mobile phone, make sure its presence is relayed in your request for the emergency services.)

Radar Balloon

There are several radar reflective balloons on the market, some of which fly like a kite, while others are gas-filled. The best of these is the Locaid, which is quick and easy to operate, and will fly in all types of weather, including strong winds. The Locaid is hand-held in a similar way to a pyro-technic flare. The safety tape is removed, allowing the balloon to be operated by the removal of a safety pin. The balloon inflates automatically in an aerodynamic shape, and then lifts off to fly at around 35 m (105 ft), where it is tethered by a line to the hand mechanism. The foil reflective balloon can be seen over 38 km (24 miles) away and will stay aloft for up to five days.

Visual and Sound Signals

These are perhaps the easiest signals to create by

using basic items from a survival kit. They can work well over long distances and, in some cases, when visibility is severely restricted.

Fire

A fire should be prepared and kept ready for lighting at the first sign of help arriving. For daytime use it is best to produce a high smoke volume by adding green vegetation to an established fire. At night, a bright clear flame is required which can be achieved by burning old, dry fuel.

Heliograph

Using the sun's reflection is an excellent way of signalling for help. If you do not possess a heliograph, any mirrored surface, such as a vanity mirror, a wristwatch or a piece of glass, will work.

Torch

At night even a small torch can be seen from a great distance in the right weather conditions. Remember to conserve your batteries for just such an event. If you have no torch, consider using the flash on a camera.

Flares

Small packs of survival flares can be purchased from most leading camping stores or chandlers. They must be used with care as they are a potential weapon. Always follow the instructions to the letter and aim the flare skywards. Any flare pistol should only be operated by a fully competent person. Once fired, the flare will reach a height of around 100 m (300 ft) and should be visible for many miles, depending on the weather conditions. Normally a red flare means help, but firing any flare in the mountains will attract attention.

Whistle

Almost every survival kit will contain a whistle and this is one device that you can use to your heart's content. Give six quick blasts one after the other, repeated after one minute.

Ground Signals

The letters and configurations shown below are used in ground-to-air recognition signals. When constructing them take into account that a pilot may be a long way off and therefore the size and background colour contrast of the signal is extremely important. This can be done by making your signals at least 5 m (15 ft) long and about 1.5 m (5 ft) wide.

I	II	F	A	N
Require a doctor and Casevac	*Need medical supplies*	*Need food and water*	*Yes (affirmative)*	*No*

△	LL	X	→	☐
Safe to land	*Everything OK*	*Unable to move*	*Moving this way*	*Need compass and map*

Black earth against light-coloured grass, or shadow created by tramping down fresh snow or laying down fir branches, will all add to the contrast.

WHEN HELP ARRIVES

Make yourself as obvious as possible. A Day-Glo panel, such as an orange survival bag, can easily be seen from the air. At night, flash a torch, but as the helicopter approaches direct the beam at the ground. This is because the crew may be using night vision goggles to improve safety, and even small external light sources shone directly at them can seriously reduce the goggles' efficiency or stop them working altogether. All search and rescue helicopters are fitted with powerful floodlighting.

Remember that a helicopter will approach a selected landing site into the wind, so stand well to the windward side of the aircraft. If you know where the helicopter is going to land, or have marked out a landing site yourself, make sure that it is as clear as possible of debris and that you have firmed any dry snow by stamping it down. Do not rush at the helicopter as it lands, but wait for a signal from the pilot or winch man indicating that it is safe to do so. Secure any loose equipment before the helicopter arrives in the hover and expect some downwash from the rotor blades. If the pick-up site is very steep or dangerous and requires a winch man to be lowered, try to prepare a belay (a firm anchor point to which something can be attached) for the winch man's use on his arrival. Carry out the winch man's instructions to the letter.